THE
CHILDREN
OF
LA SALETTE

THE
CHILDREN
OF
LA SALETTE

by
Mary Fabyan Windeatt

Illustrated by
Gedge Harmon

Nihil obstat: Joseph D. Brokage, S.T.D.
                   Censor librorum

Imprimatur: †Paul C. Schulte, D.D.
                   Archbishop of Indianapolis

                   Feast of Our Lady of La Salette
                   September 19, 1951

This book was first published in 1951 by St. Meinrad's Abbey, Inc. This TAN Books edition has been re-typeset and revised to include corrections of typographical errors and updating of punctuation, spelling and diction.

Text by Mary Fabyan Windeatt

Illustrations by Gedge Harmon

ISBN: 978-1-5051-1106-4

Cataloging-in-Publication data on file with the Library of Congress.

Printed and bound in the United States of America.

TAN Books
Charlotte, North Carolina
www.TANBooks.com
2017

To the Virgin who wept
at La Salette,
who is also
Our Lady of Lourdes,
of Fatima,
and of all the World.

Grateful acknowledgment is due the Reverend Philibert J. O'Hara, M.S., Director of the La Salette Seminary, Hartford, Connecticut, for his help and encouragement in preparing this little story.

CHAPTER ONE

I T WAS eleven o'clock in the morning of Friday, September 18, 1846, but fourteen-year-old Melanie Mathieu was scarcely interested in that. At the moment she was feeling peevish. A strange shepherd boy and his dog had just crept up behind her in a most startling way as she sat watching her master's four cows on the slopes of the French Alps near the hamlet of Ablandins. And they had caught her "talking to the flowers," a game she had liked to play since she was a small child, but one which all the other young shepherds thought silly.

"Go away, boy," she said crossly. "This isn't your field."

But the newcomer, his dark eyes sparkling with mischief, only laughed. "It's all right, little girl. I'm

Maximin Giraud and this is my dog Loulou. We've come to play with you. You see, we're from Corps, too."

Melanie jumped to her feet. What if this stupid boy (whom she had seen yesterday for the first time) did come from her own town? That was no reason to startle a person or make fun of her.

"Didn't you hear me?" she exclaimed impatiently. "I want to be left alone!" Then, as Maximin did not budge, she hurried resolutely up the steep slope to find another resting place. But she had gone only a few yards when Maximin came running after her—breathless but cheerful—accompanied by the faithful Loulou.

"What's the matter?" he demanded. "My master told me to come and watch his four cows and my goat in your field."

Melanie scowled. "Your master?"

"Yes, Peter Selme. See? He's down there on the mountain mowing hay. I've been working for him since Monday because his little girl is sick and he can't find anyone else to watch the cows."

Melanie shaded her eyes from the warm September sun. Sure enough, Peter Selme, whose field adjoined that of Baptiste Pra, her own master, was busy with his scythe far down the mountainside. But surely he hadn't told this wretched boy to bother her! Like everyone else in the neighborhood, he knew that Melanie Mathieu seldom played with other children. In fact, he probably agreed with them that she was queer and was best left to herself.

"Go away, boy," she repeated firmly. "I told you I want to be alone." And picking up her shepherd's staff, she sped still farther up the mountainside. Only when it seemed evident that Maximin and his dog were not going to follow did she come to a halt. Then, after a moment's hesitation, she sat down on the grassy turf and began talking to the flowers again—pretending that they were kind people who were her friends.

However, in just a few minutes Maximin had crept up quietly behind her and seated himself a short distance away, Loulou at his feet.

"Why don't you want to play with me?" he asked plaintively. "I promise to be very good."

Exasperated beyond words, Melanie started up the mountainside again. Yet this time Maximin followed at her heels, pleading his cause so earnestly (he had never been a shepherd before, it seemed, and was very lonely), that Melanie finally let herself be persuaded. Yes, he might stay with her—and Loulou, too—but only on certain conditions.

"You'll have to be very quiet."

"Oh, yes!"

"You mustn't make fun when I talk to the flowers."

"Of course not."

"All right, then. Sit down. But keep your eyes on the cows so they don't fall down that ravine over there."

For a while all went well. Melanie gathered daisies and other wildflowers and arranged them in colorful patterns on the grass. But when she began to talk to

"GO AWAY, BOY. I WANT TO BE ALONE."

them as though they were real people, Maximin burst out laughing.

"Silly! Flowers haven't any ears," he said. "Come on—let's play a real game."

"Maximin! You promised to be quiet!"

"I know. But I'm tired of sitting still. Besides, I want to show you some good tricks."

But Melanie was not interested in tricks. Or in games either, although she did agree to listen to Maximin's account of himself: that he was eleven years old, the son of a poor man in Corps who made wheels for wagons; that his own mother had died when he was a baby, and that his stepmother was not too kind to him; that he had never been away from home before, and that only with the greatest reluctance had his father allowed him to come to Ablandins to help Peter Selme until Sunday while the latter's little daughter was ill. In fact, he had insisted the boy take along the family dog and goat, and that he receive not only his regular wage but a goodly supply of butter and cheese as well.

"Papa thinks I'm not to be trusted," laughed Maximin, "that I'll forget to watch the cows, or else fall down the mountain and break my neck. That's why he didn't want to hire me out. But so far I've done all right."

"Well, it's not Sunday yet," observed Melanie dryly. "Don't brag too much." Then, after a moment: "What'll you do when you go back to Corps?"

"Nothing. Just amuse myself."

"Amuse yourself! But why don't you go to school if you live in town?"

"Oh, no! Papa sent me a few times, but I never stayed. You see, I hate books—and sitting still."

"You go to church, though?"

"Sometimes. But I don't like that much either. Or Catechism class with the priest."

"You know your prayers?"

"Just the Our Father and the Hail Mary."

Melanie stared at the boy beside her. How strange he was! How thin and small! Why, he seemed more like eight than eleven! And yet there was something appealing about him, too, despite his restlessness and mischievous ways. . . .

"Go on," she said, with unexpected interest. "Tell me more." But Maximin only laughed. "No, it's your turn now. What about yourself and your own family?"

A bit hesitantly Melanie consented to tell a little about herself. Her home was also in Corps (some six miles from Ablandins), but she had spent a good deal of time away from there. In fact, from the age of ten she had cared for the sheep and cattle of various farmers in the neighborhood—first at Quet, then at Sainte-Luce, and now for Baptiste Pra at Ablandins. There were two older brothers who sometimes worked away from home, too, and several younger brothers and sisters. Since the family was poor, the absence of one or more children meant a considerable saving on food bills. Then, their wages were also a help. But she herself always returned home for the winter, since it was too cold then to take an animal to pasture in the mountains.

"It's September 18 now," said Maximin. "You'll be going back to Corps in a few weeks."

"Yes, in November."

"Then what?"

"Why, I suppose I'll stay home until March."

For a moment the boy was silent. But just as he was on the point of asking more questions, there came the melodious chime of bells from the parish church of La Salette in the valley below.

"Sssh!" said Melanie quickly. "That's the noon Angelus. Take off your hat, Maximin, and raise your heart to God."

The boy obediently uncovered his head and was quiet for a little while. However, his lively spirits promptly returned when Melanie invited him to share her lunch. And he was all eagerness when she brought out a small, round loaf from her knapsack. But when she took a knife and traced a cross on the loaf, then punched a tiny hole in the center of the cross, saying: "Devil, if you are in there, come out; Lord, if You are in there, stay in!", at the same time quickly covering the hole, he burst out laughing.

"Melanie, what a silly girl you are!" he cried. "As though the Devil, or God, could be in a little loaf like that!"

Melanie was strangely silent. Nor did she argue or complain when the loaf slipped from her hands, and a mischievous kick from Maximin sent it rolling down the grassy slopes of the mountain into a deep ravine. Instead, she produced another loaf, cut a cross on it, prayed, then offered a generous portion to her companion.

"I've some cheese, too," she said, with a certain dignity.

Unabashed, and still laughing, Maximin devoured both bread and cheese with gusto. Then, at Melanie's suggestion, he climbed a short distance up the mountain and returned with his hat filled with wild fruit and berries.

"We'll eat these and then playa game," he said.

But Melanie shook her head. No, they had already played and talked enough. Now they must find their eight cows and Maximin's goat and take them to drink at the spring.

CHAPTER TWO

THE NEXT day, Saturday, the children met again on the mountain. However, this time Melanie did not try to run away. By now she had developed an odd sort of liking for Maximin, and even for Loulou, and when the cows and goat were peacefully grazing she suggested a game to help pass the time.

"Let's build a Paradise," she said. "That'll be lots of fun."

Maximin hesitated. "What's a Paradise?" he asked curiously.

Melanie stared in amazement. Every little shepherd knew that a Paradise was a two-storey structure built of stones. If the lower part was big enough, it could serve as a shelter from the wind and rain. But the upper part, small or large, with a flat slab for a roof, was always God's house. And it was always decorated with pretty leaves and flowers. Then suddenly she remembered. Maximin had never been a shepherd until now.

"Come on, I'll show you what a Paradise is," she said eagerly.

By noontime, accompanied by the excited Loulou, the children had gathered a considerable quantity of wildflowers. They had also located some stones higher up the mountain that would serve to build the Paradise. Thus, when they had said the Angelus, eaten their lunch and attended to the cows and goat, they started up the mountainside to begin their project. The work took considerable time, and after a while the two were both hot and tired, but they did not stop until the last stone was laid and the last flower in place.

"There! Isn't that pretty?" exclaimed Melanie, stepping back to admire the effect of their handiwork.

Maximin shrugged. "Yes, but I'm so tired! My eyes just won't stay open any more."

Melanie nodded sympathetically. "I know. I'm tired, too. And so is Loulou. Maybe we should take a nap."

"Yes, let's," said Maximin, stifling a yawn.

With a final glance at the Paradise, and at the eight cows and goat, peacefully grazing, the two withdrew a few steps and lay down on the grass. The September sun was warm in the cloudless sky. All was very still, and in just a little while both children were fast asleep.

It was nearly three o'clock when Melanie awoke with a start. The animals were nowhere to be seen! What if they had strayed away and fallen into the ravine?

"Maximin!" she cried, scrambling to her feet and running over to where the little boy lay deep in slumber, his dog beside him. "Wake up! The cows are gone!"

With an effort Maximin sat up, rubbing his eyes. But he soon realized what had happened. Loulou at his heels, he hurried after Melanie in search of the missing animals. How angry Peter Selme would be if anything had happened to his four cows! Why, he might give him a good beating, perhaps even refuse to pay him his week's wages, let alone the bonus of butter and cheese. . . .

But as they climbed to the top of a nearby knoll in order to have a better view of the pasture, both young shepherds gave an exclamation of relief. The cows and goat were safe and sound on the other side of the ravine!

"Thank God!" burst out Melanie at the sight of the little herd peacefully dozing in the bright September sun. "I was so afraid they'd strayed away and hurt themselves!"

Maximin also was relieved. Then, though he was still sleepy, he agreed that they ought to drive the herd to a better pasture. First, however, they would pick up their knapsacks which had been left beside the Paradise.

Without delay the two began to retrace their steps. But they had gone only a short distance when Melanie stopped short. A strange light was glowing about the Paradise, so bright that it hurt the eyes!

"Maximin!" she exclaimed, dropping her shepherd's staff in her excitement. "Look at that light!"

Maximin, two or three steps behind, his own staff firmly in hand, came hurrying forward. "What light? Where?"

"Down there! Don't you see?" Then, in sudden awe: "Oh, my God!"

The boy stopped, stared, then spoke reassuringly. "Don't be frightened, Melanie. And pick up your staff. If that light does anything to hurt us, I'll give it a good whack."

Then, as the two gazed at the light, it seemed to open and a smaller light appeared in its midst. This second light was even brighter than the first and whirling constantly, so that the children could not look at it for any length of time but had to stop and rub their eyes, then steal another glance. Suddenly, without warning, the strange radiance began to expand, and as it grew in dimensions they made out the faint outline of a figure—first hands covering a face, then forearms and elbows, finally a high, fluted headdress. As they stared in stupefied silence, a woman's stately figure seemed to rise from a sitting position on the Paradise. Folding her arms in her wide sleeves she moved towards them, following the zigzag course of a little brook which ran nearby.

"Come near, my children," she said gently. "And don't be afraid. I am here to tell you great news."

No longer frightened, the two youngsters hurried across the brook and took up their stand before the newcomer—Maximin on her left, Melanie on her right. And gradually their dazzled eyes perceived that the strange lady was very tall and splendidly arrayed—her dress of glittering white strewn with pearls, a large white kerchief bordered with multicolored roses draped about her shoulders, a golden apron about her waist. A braided golden chain also hung low on her shoulders, while a second and smaller golden chain hung about her neck. From this was suspended an eight-inch crucifix, with a hammer on one crossbar and pincers on the other. But majestic though she was, the lady seemed to be in great distress. Indeed, tears welled from her eyes as she gazed upon the little shepherds and began to speak:

"If my people will not submit, I shall be forced to let go the hand of my Son. It is so strong, so heavy, that I can no longer withhold it. How long a time have I suffered for you! If I would not have my Son abandon you, I am compelled to pray to Him without ceasing. And as to you, you take no heed of it. However much you pray, however much you do, you will never recompense the pains I have taken for you. Six days have I given you to labor, the seventh I have kept for myself, and they will not give it to me. Those who drive the carts cannot swear without introducing the name of my Son.

"These are the two things which make the hand of my Son so heavy. If the harvest is spoiled, it is all on your account. I gave you warning last year in the potatoes, but you did not heed it. On the contrary, when you found the potatoes spoiled, you swore, you took the name of my Son in vain. They will continue to decay, so that by Christmas there will be none left."

Awed beyond words, the children listened in bewilderment to everything the lady said. But as she spoke in French, Melanie had difficulty in following her. Of course French was the official language of the country, but the little girl had never learned it properly. Like everyone else in the neighborhood, she spoke the local peasant dialect which was a mixture of French and Italian. But Maximin (having lived all his life in Corps) had picked up some French, and Melanie was on the point of asking him to explain certain words when the lady seemed to sense her trouble.

"Ah, my children, you don't understand," she said. "Well, I shall say it in a different way." And without the slightest hesitation, she began to speak in the local dialect:

"If you have wheat, it is not good to sow it. All that you sow will fall into dust. There will come a great famine. Before the famine comes, the children under seven years of age will be seized with trembling and will die in the hands of those who hold them; and others will do penance by famine. The walnuts will become bad, the grapes will rot."

Then a strange thing happened. The lady continued speaking, but Melanie could no longer hear a word. It was as though she had suddenly become deaf. Yet the lady *was* speaking—her head turned a little toward Maximin, the tears still flowing from her eyes.

"What is it?" thought the fourteen-year-old girl. "Why can't I hear anymore?"

Then she looked at Maximin. He was all attention, although as usual he was finding it hard to keep still. Even as the lady was speaking, he had taken off his hat and was twirling it round and round on his shepherd's staff. And kicking pebbles with his feet. But dazzled though he was, he was trying to keep his eyes on the lady's face. And there was no doubt about it. He was hearing and understanding everything that was being said.

CHAPTER THREE

FOR SEVERAL minutes the lady continued to speak to Maximin. Then presently she turned to Melanie.

"What I am about to tell you is a secret," she said. "You must not breathe a word of it to anyone."

The child's heart beat with excitement. She could hear again! She understood perfectly what the lady was saying, and that it must be kept a secret! Then after a moment, including both youngsters in her gaze, the lady spoke again:

"If people are converted, the stones will be changed into heaps of wheat and the potatoes will sow themselves in the fields . . . Do you say your prayers well, my children?"

The two looked at each other, at the lady, then shook their heads. "No, not very well, Madame."

"Ah, but you *must* say them well, my children, morning and evening. At least an Our Father and a Hail Mary, when you cannot do better or say more."

Then, before the little shepherds could promise to mend their ways, she continued:

"In summer only a few old women go to Mass; the rest work on Sundays all summer; and in winter, when they don't know what to do, they go to Mass only to make fun of religion. During Lent, they go to the meat market like dogs."

The children were silent. How true it all was! And yet, what could they do about it? Everyone worked on Sunday. Of course it was actually the Lord's Day and therefore should be given to prayer. But there was *so* much to be done if one lived on a farm! And even if one lived in a town like Corps there was almost as much, especially if one owned a shop. Why, usually there was more business on Sunday than on any other day of the week! People flocked to the stores to do their shopping after Mass. And to the taverns, too.

The lady seemed to sense the children's thoughts. "Have you ever seen wheat that is spoiled?" she asked.

Maximin shook his head vigorously. "No, Madame."

The lady looked closely at the little boy. "But, my child, you surely saw it once, with your father, near Coin. The owner of the field told your father to go and see his ruined wheat. You went both together. You took two or three ears into your hands and rubbed them, and they fell into dust. Then you returned home. When you were still half an hour's distance

"DO YOU SAY YOUR PRAYERS WELL, MY CHILDREN?"

from Corps, your father gave you a piece of bread and said to you: 'Here, my child, eat some bread this year at least; I don't know who will eat any next year, if the wheat goes on like that.'"

Maximin shifted awkwardly. He had forgotten all about this particular event. "Oh, yes, Madame," he said quickly. "I remember now. Just a moment ago I didn't recall."

The lady readily understood a lapse of memory. Turning suddenly, and once again speaking in French instead of the local dialect, she stepped lightly across the brook. "Well, my children, you will make this known to all my people," she said. And having repeated these words in a kind and motherly voice, she started up the mountainside.

With a sinking heart Melanie realized what was about to happen. The beautiful stranger was preparing to leave! Quickly she hurried after her, noting as she did so that there were square golden buckles on the lady's white shoes, also pearls, that she wore gold-colored stockings, and that the soles of her shoes were edged with roses. But even more surprising was the fact that she seemed to walk on top of the grass blades without bending them, as though she were floating, and that the roses on her shoes were not crushed by her steps. Then, too, though the September sun was bright, neither the lady, Maximin nor Melanie herself cast any shadow.

There was no time to ponder this, however. The lady had almost reached the little knoll where just a short time before the children had spied their missing cattle. Scarcely knowing what she did, Melanie took a short cut and ran ahead, eager to feast her eyes on the lady's shining beauty and to hear her speak again. Maximin, staff in hand, hastily brought up the rear. But apparently the lady had no more to say. Her hands folded in the long, wide sleeves of her beautiful dress (as they had been all during her visit), she looked fondly at the two little shepherds on either side of her. Then she began to rise slowly into the air. When she had reached a point some four or five feet above the earth, she began to disappear. First her head faded from their sight, then the rest of her body, down to her feet. At last only a strange brilliance remained where she had been, and this vanished almost instantly.

For a time the two children could only gaze at the place in bewilderment. Then, little by little, they came to themselves, a dozen questions upon their lips. Who was the beautiful lady? Where did she live? Why had she come? How could she vanish so strangely, almost as though she had melted away? And Loulou, who was such a good watchdog, why hadn't she barked at the beautiful stranger?

"Maximin, maybe it was a great saint!" exclaimed Melanie.

The boy's eyes clouded with dismay. "Why didn't we think to ask?" he blurted out. "Oh, Melanie, if the lady really came from heaven she could have taken us with her when she went back. . . ."

For several minutes the children continued to discuss the recent marvel. Then, puzzled and cast down, they went in search of the cows. But soon Maximin had regained some of his usual light-heartedness.

"Melanie, once the lady stopped talking to the two of us and talked just to you," he remarked curiously. "I couldn't hear a word, but I could see her lips moving. What did she say?"

Melanie felt her heart give a great leap. So, for a little while, Maximin had been deaf, too? But she shook her head quickly. "No, I can't tell you what the lady said. It's a secret."

The boy laughed, and flung a stick for Loulou to chase. "Well, she told me a secret, too," he remarked, a trifle boastfully. "And I'm not going to breathe a word about it either. But I do wish. . . ."

"What?"

"That we knew who she was."

For a few more minutes the children continued their pondering. But as the sun began to go down behind the mountains and a chill wind sprang up, they gathered the herd together and drove them down to the valley. Then they parted—Melanie for the house of Baptiste Pra, Maximin to find Peter Selme.

CHAPTER FOUR

MELANIE HAD every intention of telling the Pra family of what had happened on the mountainside. But when she arrived home, she decided to finish certain chores first. For instance, the cows had to be milked and bedded down for the night. Then, there was the usual amount of cleaning up to be done in the stable. But although she worked as fast as she could, the little girl made only slow progress. Then presently she burst into bitter tears. How sad the beautiful lady had been! How grieved because people cursed and swore and did not keep Sunday as they should. . . .

"Melanie, child! What is it?" asked a quavering voice suddenly. "What happened to you this afternoon on the mountain?"

Melanie looked up. Old Madame Pra, Baptiste's mother, was standing in the shadows by the stable door, tears streaming down her withered cheeks.

Quickly the fourteen-year-old girl brushed away her own tears and came forward. "N-nothing, Madame."

"Nothing? But Maximin's been telling us that the Blessed Virgin appeared to you! And he says . . . oh, child, forget about the chores and come in the house at once!"

Her head in a whirl, Melanie obeyed. How was it that Maximin wasn't at Peter Selme's house having his supper? And as for the lady's being the Blessed Virgin. . . .

Soon the whole story was out. Maximin had met Peter Selme on the road and told him everything. But after arriving home he could find no one else to talk to, and so he had hurried over to the Pra house. And it was old Madame Pra, then her daughter-in-law, Baptiste's wife, who had decided that the beautiful stranger was none other than the Mother of God, and that dreadful things were in store for everyone because of the apparition.

"Melanie, begin at the beginning!" urged the terrified old lady. "And Maximin, you help her out if she forgets anything."

Melanie looked doubtfully at Maximin, who, quite at his ease, was sitting beside Baptiste's wife at the kitchen table. "How much did you tell?" she asked.

The boy shrugged. "All I could remember. But do what Madame Pra says, Melanie, because I probably left out a few little things."

So, in the warmth of the comfortable kitchen (where preparations for the evening meal had been quite forgotten), Melanie began to describe what had happened in the pasture—the glowing light above the Paradise, the lady and her beautiful dress, her tears, her message. However, halfway through the story, Baptiste Pra and his brother James returned from the fields and it was necessary to start all over again. But finally everything was told, and there was silence in the kitchen, broken only by the sobs of Madame Pra and her daughter-in-law.

"The lady was the Blessed Virgin!" the two women insisted tearfully. "And she's angry with us because of our sins! Oh, what'll we do?"

Baptiste Pra, undecided as to believe the children's story or not, hurriedly made the Sign of the Cross. "Maximin, go and tell Peter Selme to come over after supper," he said gruffly. "This is terribly serious."

Then, as Maximin reluctantly took his departure: "Melanie, the lady was very sad? She was crying all the time she spoke to you?"

The little girl nodded. "Yes, sir. Nearly all the time, especially when she talked about people working on Sunday. And all the swearing they do."

"What were her exact words again?"

"'Six days have I given you to labor, the seventh I have kept for myself, and they will not give it to me. Those who drive the carts cannot swear without introducing the name of my Son. These are the two things which make the hand of my Son so heavy.'"

Old Madame Pra wiped away her tears with a shaking hand. "She spoke about famine, too, didn't she, child?"

"Yes. She especially mentioned the lack of potatoes."

"It's true! They've been rotting all summer!" sobbed Baptiste's wife.

"Well, they're going to keep on rotting, Madame. There won't be any left by Christmas. As for the wheat—"

"Yes, yes! What did she say about that?"

"'If you have wheat, it is not good to sow it. All that you sow will fall into dust. There will come a great famine. Before the famine comes, the children under seven years of age will be seized with trembling and will die in the hands of those who hold them; and others will do penance by famine. The walnuts will become bad, the grapes will rot.'"

At this there was a fresh outburst of weeping on the part of the two women. Famine and death—perhaps this very winter!

However, James Pra, Baptiste's younger brother, was openly scornful of the whole affair. "Why do we have to believe what Melanie says?" he demanded. "That child hardly knows her prayers! And look at all the times we've had to scold her for being lazy and careless at her work! Do you think the Blessed Virgin would appear to a little girl like that?"

Melanie hung her head. Her master's brother spoke only the truth. And yet—

"I know I've been bad sometimes," she muttered. "But I'm sorry, sir. And *please* believe me now!"

Even as she was speaking, there was a commotion outside. Peter Selme, his family and several neighbors had arrived at the Pra house, troubled beyond words. To think that possibly the Blessed Virgin had visited among them just a few hours ago! Even more. That she was displeased with everyone who worked on Sundays or used bad language, and that unless these people mended their ways and did penance, terrible things were going to happen. . . .

"It's as though the good God Himself had been here," muttered Peter fearfully. Then, after a moment: "I'm surely one of those sinners the Blessed Virgin meant. Why, I had every intention of going out in the fields tomorrow—even if it is Sunday!"

"So had I," admitted Baptiste Pra. "The hay is just right for cutting. But maybe now. . . ."

"Now you'll say your prayers and spend the rest of the day as it should be spent," said his wife. "And so will I."

"And the young ones—what about them?"

"Why, they'll do like the rest of us, of course."

"I mean these young ones, Melanie and Maximin. The Blessed Virgin, if that's who it was, told them to . . . what was it she said, Melanie?"

"'Well, my children, you will make this known to all my people.' She said that twice, sir, just before she left us."

"That's what I thought. 'All my people.' Well, that could mean. . . ."

"Yes, sir?"

"That you're to go to all the countries in the world with this message."

Melanie's heart sank. How could two children undertake such a stupendous task all by themselves? But to her amazement, Maximin was not at all disturbed. In fact, the thought of going around the world immediately caught his fancy.

"We'd be like priests, Melanie!" he burst out excitedly. "We'd give sermons in church and everyone would be converted. People wouldn't work on Sundays any more, or swear either. My, how nice it would be!"

But after a moment's reflection, Baptiste Pra shook his head. What foolish talk! Of course nothing could be decided before the children had seen and spoken with Father James Perrin, the parish priest of La Salette.

"You'd better go to the rectory before Mass tomorrow and tell him what's happened," he announced. "That old man's a good and holy priest. He'll know whether we should believe all this or not."

CHAPTER FIVE

BEFORE DAWN the next day Melanie and Maximin were on the road to La Salette, a mile or so distant from Ablandins. But they had not gone very far when they met the town policeman.

"And where are you off to so early in the morning?" he demanded curiously. "Shouldn't you be busy with your chores?"

Maximin's eyes sparkled. "Oh, no, sir! We have to see Father Perrin and tell him how the Blessed Virgin appeared to us yesterday."

Melanie nodded. "That's right. We want to know what to do about her message."

The policeman gaped. *"What?"*

At once the two children began to explain what had happened. The Blessed Virgin (they were sure of this now) had appeared to them yesterday afternoon while they were watching their cattle. She was very sad because people worked on Sundays and used bad language. Unless there was a change, terrible things were going to happen.

"She said to make this known to everyone, sir," explained Melanie. "And our masters think we should see Father Perrin right away."

"That's why we're out so early," put in Maximin eagerly. "We want to talk to him before Mass."

For a moment the policeman said nothing. Then his eyes began to twinkle. "That's a good one!" he chuckled. "The Blessed Virgin leaves the glories of heaven to talk to two poor youngsters in a cow pasture! And right in our own neighborhood, too! Well, well, wait'll I tell this to the Mayor!" Then, shaking a playful finger at the children: "It's a good story, little ones, but you'd better be careful. Don't you know it's a serious thing to spread lies and gossip? Why, you could go to jail for less than that!"

As the policeman moved down the street, Melanie's heart grew heavy. How dreadful if others didn't believe their story!

Maximin seemed to read her thoughts. "Never mind," he said consolingly. "It'll be different when we've explained things to Father Perrin."

"Y-yes," murmured the little girl. "I suppose it will." Then, a trifle more cheerfully: "Come on. We'd better hurry up if we want to see him."

A few minutes later they had reached the rectory and were knocking hopefully at the door.

"We'd like to talk to Father Perrin, please," Melanie informed the housekeeper. "We've something very important to tell him."

The housekeeper, a stout, rather stern-faced woman in her middle forties, looked the two children up and down, then shook her head firmly. "Father's writing his Sunday sermon now and can't be bothered," she declared. "What is it you want?"

Remembering how the policeman had made light of the story of the apparition, Melanie hesitated. "We ... we'd rather not tell you, Madame. It's something only the priest can help us with. Please, couldn't we see him for a few minutes?"

The housekeeper snorted. "Didn't you hear me, little girl? Father Perrin's busy. And I can't stand here all day. What's the matter?"

Only the fact that she had been ordered by Baptiste Pra to speak to the parish priest made Melanie hold her ground. She must see Father Perrin. That was all there was to it.

"Well, well, all right," grumbled the housekeeper. "Come around to the kitchen and we'll see what can be done."

Once the children were seated in the kitchen, however, the housekeeper fell prey to curiosity. It was certainly odd that Baptiste Pra and Peter Selme should send these youngsters to see Father Perrin at such an early hour. Had they been especially bad? Or was there some kind of trouble brewing in either household?

"Come, now," she coaxed. "What is it, children? Surely you can tell me what's on your mind, especially if it'll save time for the good priest. He's a busy man on Sundays, you know. And none too well these days. . . ."

Maximin shrugged as Melanie's troubled eyes met his. "Tell her," he urged. "After all, the Blessed Virgin did say to make her words known to everyone."

So once again Melanie began the familiar story. Then, after a moment—

"That's all, Madame. After about half an hour the Blessed Virgin rose up in the air and disappeared. But just before she did that, she told us to make her words known to all the people. That's why we're here this morning—to ask Father Perrin what to do."

The housekeeper was staring at them in blank astonishment. Then suddenly she recovered herself. "But this is impossible!" she burst out. "Why, the Blessed Virgin would never show herself to the likes of you—two little shepherds who haven't even made your First Communion!"

Maximin quivered with excitement. "But she did!" he insisted eagerly. "And it was so nice seeing her, Madame! She wore the prettiest white dress, all shiny with pearls, and a gold apron over it. And there were roses around the edges of her shoes—blue and pink and white and red—"

The housekeeper frowned. "What nonsense, lad! Who ever heard of blue roses? Now if you've made up this whole thing. . . ."

"YOU'D BETTER BE CAREFUL!"

Melanie shook her head vigorously. "He's not made up anything, Madame. The Blessed Virgin did have blue roses around her shoes. And around her head-dress, too. And each flower had a beautiful light in its center. . . ."

Then suddenly she broke off. Old Father Perrin, the parish priest of La Salette, had appeared in the kitchen doorway—tears streaming down his kindly face.

"Children, I've heard it all!" he stammered. "Famine! Sickness! Death! Oh, my God, what's going to become of us?"

Then, to Melanie's amazement, he reached out a trembling hand. "Come into my study, little ones. Tell me everything again. And slowly, slowly, so that I can write it down. . . ."

CHAPTER SIX

SOON THE two had related the familiar story once again, while the parish priest, deeply moved, made notes of all that was said.

"This will be my sermon for today," he declared. "Please God that it touches many hearts. . . ."

There was a moment's silence, during which Melanie looked doubtfully at Maximin. Father Perrin seemed to have forgotten all about them now and was gazing fixedly at the sheets of paper in his trembling hands. And as yet he had not given them any advice.

"Father, what do you want us to do?" she ventured finally.

With an effort the priest gave the children his attention. "*Do?* Ah, pray, little ones! And never forget you've had the great privilege of seeing the Mother of God."

Maximin shifted uneasily. "Then you don't want us anymore, Father? We can go home now?"

The priest nodded. "Yes, child. I guess it's best that you leave me. You see, I have to think." Then, after a moment's hesitation: "It might be well to go and see Father Mélin, the parish priest of Corps. He's a wise man, little ones. He'll be able to give you good advice."

The two nodded silently. Then, after a brief farewell with the housekeeper (who now treated them with respect and was bursting with questions), they took their departure. As they stepped outside, a quick glance at the sky told Melanie that the sun must have risen over an hour ago, but a chill wind had sprung up and heavy clouds were gathering over the mountains.

"Maximin, let's stay for Mass," she suggested. "It's going to rain, so we won't have to take the cows to pasture."

The boy shook his head. "Don't you remember? This is the day Peter Selme takes me back to Corps. He told me to come straight home after I'd seen the priest."

Melanie's eyes clouded with disappointment. For the moment she had forgotten that Maximin's week of service was over. She would not be seeing him again, at least not until November when she herself returned to Corps.

"All right," she agreed reluctantly. "Well, good-bye, Maximin. I hope you don't get caught in the storm."

The boy laughed. "It doesn't matter if I am," he said. "Peter Selme will look after me." And with a brief wave of his hand, he took to his heels and was off in the direction of Ablandins.

For several minutes Melanie wandered aimlessly about the churchyard. Then, as people began to arrive for the parish Mass, she went inside and took a place near the door. This, she reflected, was really a great day. Seldom did she have the opportunity to hear Mass, for her work with the cattle kept her away from church even on Sundays. Then, too, how splendid to think that in a little while Father Perrin would be telling everyone about Our Lady's message!

"I wonder what he'll say," she mused. "And if the people will be very much surprised."

It was immediately after the Gospel that the old pastor mounted the pulpit and began to describe Our Lady's apparition on the mountain—her sorrow at the way people cursed, swore and did unnecessary work on Sundays. But from the beginning his voice was so choked with emotion that Melanie could scarcely understand what he was saying. Then, too, remembering her part in the whole affair, she had the unreasonable fear that someone might turn around and recognize her. Thus, as soon as Mass was over, she hurried out of church. Despite the prospect of a rainy day, she had hopes of visiting the mountain where the Blessed Virgin had shown herself the previous afternoon.

"Maybe she'll come again!" thought the little girl eagerly. "Oh, how wonderful that would be!"

However, when she reached home and asked Baptiste Pra's permission to make the trip, the latter shook his head. The weather was too bad, he declared. It would be far better if Melanie made herself useful about the house. She could spend some time in prayer, too, since that would surely please the Blessed Virgin.

"Yes, sir," said Melanie, a bit disappointed. "But I can go tomorrow, can't I?" Baptiste hesitated. "Well, maybe—if it isn't raining too much."

The little girl controlled her impatience as best she could. Indeed, the members of the Pra family kept her busy for most of the day with new questions about her great experience, and the time passed rapidly Then, in the late afternoon, a carriage drew up at the door.

Old Madame Pra hobbled to the window. "It's Mayor Peytard from La Salette!" she exclaimed excitedly. "My, my, Melanie, he's probably come to talk to you!"

True enough. The policeman whom the children had met early that morning had given the Mayor a partial account of their story. Then there had been Father Perrin's sermon. But this had been delivered under such great stress of feeling that few in the congregation had a clear notion of what had been said. Besides, the Mayor was not a man to be easily convinced. He must see Baptiste Pra's young shepherdess himself.

"Come, little girl, what's all this about?" he demanded impatiently, scarcely taking time to settle himself in a chair. "You don't mean to say you actually saw the Blessed Virgin yesterday? And spoke with her, too?"

Melanie nodded calmly. "Yes, sir."

"Nonsense! You had a dream, that's all."

"Oh, no, sir. It wasn't a dream. Maximin saw her, too."

"Humph! And what did Our Lady have to say?"

"A good deal, sir. But the most important part was that people shouldn't use bad language, or keep Sunday like an ordinary day. If they do, terrible things will happen."

The Mayor scowled. "What, for instance?"

"Famine, sir. And then a plague."

There was silence for a moment. Then the Mayor sprang up and began to pace the room. "I'm no fool, little girl!" he roared. "And I've a good mind to put you in jail for such foolish talk. Come, now—tell me the truth. You and Maximin made up this whole story, didn't you, just to make yourselves seem important?"

Melanie turned pale. How angry the Mayor was! And what a terribly loud voice he had! Why, old Madame Pra and her daughter-in-law looked frightened to death. . . .

"Speak up, child," urged Baptiste Pra anxiously. "If you've lied to us, it's much better to say so now. But if you keep on with your lies. . . ."

Suddenly new courage came to Melanie. "But I'm *not* lying!" she burst out indignantly. "The Blessed Virgin really did come yesterday. And she said exactly what I've told you."

Once again there was silence. Then the Mayor changed his course. The hardness went out of his eyes and his voice softened. "Look, my dear," he said, taking Melanie's hand, "suppose we forget about this whole thing. Here are twenty francs. Keep this money. It's all yours. But first promise me not to say another word about what happened yesterday. That's a bargain, isn't it?"

Melanie stared. Twenty francs (four dollars) was more money than her father made in a week of hard work! But not to talk any more about the Blessed Virgin's visit? Not to obey her command to make her words known to everyone?

"Oh, sir, I couldn't promise that!" she exclaimed. "I just couldn't!" Then, as the Mayor tried to press the twenty francs more firmly into her hand: "No, no, sir! I wouldn't disobey Our Lady . . . not for a whole house full of money!"

CHAPTER SEVEN

FOR A good three hours Mayor Peytard did his best to make Melanie change her story—by threats, new bribes and coaxing of all sorts. But to no avail.

"That child is telling the truth," he finally confided to Baptiste Pra as the latter escorted him to his carriage. "I'm sure of it."

"I'm sure of it, too, sir," agreed Baptiste, who, although distressed because of Melanie's long ordeal, also realized that the Mayor was a good man and had not meant to be cruel in his method of questioning. "But what's to be done now?"

For a moment the Mayor was thoughtful. "I think I'll go to Corps tomorrow and talk to Maximin," he said finally. "And if *he* doesn't break down either—well, you and I had better go to the holy mountain, my friend, and pray as we've never prayed before."

When the Mayor reached home that night, however, with a full account of what had taken place at Baptiste Pra's house in Ablandins, his wife was not at all impressed.

"Melanie Mathieu's just an ignorant little girl," she declared indignantly. "As for Maximin Giraud, surely the Blessed Virgin would never appear to the likes of him."

"And why not?"

"Because of his father, of course."

"His father? Why, what's his father got to do with it?"

"Haven't you heard? He's a drunkard, that's what. He spends more time in the tavern than anywhere else. Why, he even takes Maximin there and encourages him to drink, too. And they do say—"

"Yes?"

"Well . . . that Giraud has taught the boy to smoke!"

The Mayor's eyes shot open with astonishment. "Maximin smokes? Oh, no! Why, he's only eleven!"

"No matter, he smokes. And he uses coarse language, too. But what else could you expect, with bad example all around him? Maybe it would have been different if his mother had lived, but that stepmother of his—why, she scarcely gives the lad enough to eat! No wonder he's an ill-mannered little ruffian who won't go to school or to church."

The Mayor listened attentively to all that his wife had to say. But the next day, Monday, when he went to Corps, he was agreeably surprised. Maximin, although lively and restless, was courteous and eager to answer every question put to him. And with such sincerity and exactness that the Mayor was impressed in spite of himself. And when the boy refused, like Melanie, to change even the smallest part of his story because of threats, bribes or coaxing, the Mayor abruptly ended the interview and returned to La Salette in a sober mood.

"The Blessed Virgin *must* have shown herself to these children," he reflected. "There are no two ways about it."

By the end of the day many others were of the same opinion, especially when it became known that a spring, long dry, had now reappeared on the very spot where the children had first seen Our Lady. Of course there were scoffers who insisted that Sunday's heavy rain had caused the sudden flow of water, and that in time it would dry up. Nevertheless, by Tuesday morning several pious souls had already gone to see the place for themselves, to drink from the spring and to say their prayers beside it.

"Fools!" exclaimed Maximin's father when he heard the news. "And to think you helped start all this commotion, boy! Aren't you ashamed of yourself?"

Maximin shook his head vigorously. "Oh, no, Papa. And look—you must believe about Our Lady's visit! You see, she talked quite a lot about you."

Giraud stared. *"Me?"*

"Yes. She asked Melanie and me if we'd ever seen any wheat that was spoiled, and I said we hadn't. Then she reminded me that I'd seen some that day you took me with you to Coin."

At these words, a peculiar expression crossed Giraud's face. "Really?" he asked sharply. "What exactly did she say?"

Maximin was quick to take advantage of his father's interest. "All right, Papa. This *is* exactly what Our Lady said:

"The owner of the field told your father to go and see his ruined wheat. You went both together. You took two or three ears into your hands and rubbed them, and they fell into dust. Then you returned home. When you were still half an hour's distance from Corps, your father gave you a piece of bread and said to you: 'Here, my child, eat some bread this year at least; I don't know who will eat any next year, if the wheat goes on like that.'"

Maximin's father was all attention now. How well he remembered this particular incident! But how was it possible, since no one else had been around at the time. . . .

"Well, Papa, now do you believe that the lady was the Blessed Virgin?" asked Maximin eagerly.

Giraud hesitated. A young scatterbrain such as Maximin would never have recalled all this by himself. And with such amazing accuracy. Why, it had taken three to four years just to teach him the Our Father

A MIRACULOUS SPRING HAD APPEARED!

and the Hail Mary! And now, without the slightest trouble, he could repeat long speeches made by the lady—either in French, which he scarcely knew, or in the local dialect. And from all accounts Melanie could do the same, although she knew no French at all.

"I . . . I guess so," he admitted. "There's not much else to do."

As a result of this story about the spoiled wheat, life at home suddenly became much more pleasant for Maximin. His stepmother no longer mistreated him, or scoffed at reports of the vision. Indeed, she was all eagerness to visit the holy mountain. His grandmother, too, was in favor of the idea. As for his little cousin, ten-year-old Melanie Carnal, who had been suffering from a serious eye infection for a long time, she could hardly wait to make the six-mile pilgrimage.

"Go ahead and take the child," said Maximin's father one morning. "It can't do any harm."

"Of course you're coming, too," said Madame Giraud. "Perhaps the Blessed Virgin will cure your asthma if you pray to her on the mountain."

But this was too much for Maximin's father. What would his friends at the tavern say if they heard he had gone on a pilgrimage with pious womenfolk? Already he had had to put up with a good deal of ridicule because of Maximin's part in the recent events. Besides, it was many months since he had even entered a church, let alone received the Sacraments. . . .

"No, no," he said hastily. "I haven't time for anything like that." Then, after a moment: "Just one thing, though."

"Yes?"

"Take a good look around the mountain when you're there. See if there's not some place where this . . . this lady could have hidden before the children saw her."

"You mean you still think it could have been a stranger pretending to be the Blessed Virgin?"

"I'm not saying. But it certainly won't do any harm to look about."

So presently the group set forth—Maximin, his stepmother, his grandmother, Melanie Carnal and several neighbors—while Giraud stood watching with mixed feelings.

"It's just a waste of time," mocked a little voice deep in his heart. *"This is the nineteenth century, my friend. Miracles don't happen these modern days."*

But then came another voice, far more insistent: *"If my people will not submit, I shall be forced to let go the hand of my Son. It is so strong, so heavy, that I can no longer withhold it. . . ."*

CHAPTER EIGHT

WHEN THE pilgrims returned to the Giraud house that night, there was great rejoicing. Young Melanie Carnal was no longer suffering from her eye trouble! The painful infection, though its traces remained, had been wonderfully relieved through Our Lady's intercession.

"It's true!" Madame Giraud told her husband excitedly. "The child bathed her eyes at the miraculous spring, and in a few minutes—well, just look at her now!"

Maximin's father looked. The little girl's eyes were entirely normal, save for a slight redness about the rims.

"T-that's fine," he muttered doubtfully. "Just fine."

Melanie nodded eagerly. "The Blessed Virgin did it, sir! She's ever so much better than a doctor. You'll have to go and see her about your asthma."

"Yes, Papa," put in Maximin. "She'll fix you up in no time."

Giraud shrugged impatiently. "You did what I told you to?" he demanded of his wife.

At this Madame Giraud could no longer restrain her annoyance. "Unbeliever! Of course I did!" she burst out. "And there's absolutely no place where anyone could have hidden in order to fool the children. No trees, bushes, nothing. Everything Maximin's told us is true. The Blessed Virgin did show herself on the mountain, and I'm going there again the first chance I get."

"So am I," announced the boy's grandmother. "It's a holy place, Giraud, and you were a fool not to have gone with us today. Why, you might have been helped, too, just like Melanie was!"

"Never mind, he'll be going there this very week," declared Madame Giraud firmly. "I'll see to that."

Of course there was great excitement in Corps when word of what had happened to Melanie Carnal became general knowledge. Scores of new pilgrims, many in poor health, set out to visit the holy mountain carrying jars, crocks and other containers in which to bring back water from the miraculous spring.

No one was more interested in what was going on than Father Mélin, the parish priest of Corps. "The Mayor of La Salette has already questioned the children," he reflected. "Maybe I'd better do the same." Then, after a pause: "I'll start with Maximin, since he lives here. Perhaps later on I'll find time to go to Ablandins to see Melanie Mathieu."

Saturday, September 26, the octave of the apparition, was the day set for the interview. But it was
not only Maximin who arrived at the rectory then.
Melanie was also on hand, for that morning she had
come into Corps for a visit with her family.

As usual, the two youngsters answered all the
questions put to them with eagerness and dispatch.
Yes, the Blessed Virgin had been very tall and beautiful, like a queen. Her face and garments had shone
more brightly than the sun. For a moment the two of
them had been terrified by this brilliance. Then Our
Lady had spoken in such kind and motherly tones
that they had all but flown to her side. Melanie had
stood on her right, Maximin on her left, and so dose
that no one could have passed between them and Our
Lady. But oh, how sad she had been because of all the
sins people were committing!

"The swearing, Father—it makes her feel terrible!"

"And the working on Sundays."

"And not keeping Lent properly."

"And missing Mass."

"And behaving badly in church."

Father Mélin nodded understandingly. "Yes, yes,
little ones. I know all that. But what else did Our Lady
say? Tell me everything. *Everything,* understand? It's
most important that you keep nothing back."

Melanie looked uneasily at Maximin. "But we can't
do that, Father," she objected. "It . . . it wouldn't be
right."

"Why not?"

"Because Our Lady gave each of us a secret, and we mustn't tell them to anyone."

"That's right," put in Maximin hurriedly. "I don't know Melanie's and she doesn't know mine. And she's not going to know it either."

Father Mélin stared. What was this? *Two heavenly secrets?* Then slowly a smile spread across his face. "Well, you can tell your secrets to me," he said encouragingly. "I'm a priest, you know—your own pastor—and I won't breathe a word of what you say to anyone."

But the two shook their heads. They could not share their secrets. They would rather die than disobey the Blessed Virgin, who was so kind and beautiful and good.

In spite of himself, Father Mélin was impressed. "Children, I want you to come with me tomorrow to the holy mountain and explain just what happened," he said finally. "And don't worry. I won't trouble you again about the secrets. I just want you to show me where you took your naps, where you first saw Our Lady sitting down, the place she disappeared, and so forth. You'll do that, won't you?"

The children hesitated. Then Melanie made up her mind. "Not tomorrow, Father. But maybe the day after."

"And why not tomorrow?"

"Because we promised the Mayor of La Salette to go with him then. He wants to ask more questions, too."

True enough. On Sunday morning, in company with the chief of police of Corps and several other important townsfolk, Maximin was brought to the Mayor's house in La Salette. Here Melanie joined the party, after which all set out on the one-mile trip to the place of the apparition. However, on reaching the holy mountain the children were not only required to repeat their now familiar story, but to reenact it as well. And so convincing was their performance that presently every doubt had vanished from the minds of those present.

But Mayor Peytard had one more test in store for them. As it came time to return to Corps, he motioned the chief of police aside. "You've got the rope ready?" he whispered.

The latter nodded briskly. "Yes, right under my coat."

"Very well. Call the boy. And put on the best act you can. Remember, there's a good deal at stake."

With a flourish the chief of police brought forth a length of stout rope. "Maximin!" he roared. "Where are you?"

There was no reply, for Maximin was once again up the mountainside explaining certain details of Our Lady's apparition to a little group of interested pilgrims. But soon he came running.

"Yes, sir? You wanted me?"

The policeman's face was stern as he uncoiled his rope. "That's right, boy. Ah, you thought you had us fooled, didn't you?"

"Fooled, sir? I . . . I don't understand."

"All this nonsense about the Blessed Virgin! Ha, did you really think we believed it?"

"But it's true! She *did* come. . . ."

"Silence!" cried the policeman, seizing Maximin in an iron grip. "Confess this whole business is a lie, young man, or I'll tie you up and drag you off to jail this very minute. Hurry up, now! We've wasted enough time already." Then, as an excited murmur ran through the crowd: "Friends, Maximin here has something to say to us—something very important."

For a moment no one spoke. The Mayor, the chief of police, the various pilgrims and officials—all gazed expectantly at the small, pale-faced boy before them. Melanie, too, trembling like a leaf, stood waiting.

"Go on, speak up!" snapped the Mayor. "We can't stay here all day."

Maximin shifted awkwardly. Then slowly he shook his head. "Everything I said was true," he muttered. "Our Lady did come, right over there by the spring like I told you."

At these words fresh courage filled Melanie's heart. "That's so!" she burst out tearfully. "And no matter what you do to us, we can't ever say anything else!"

CHAPTER NINE

A SIGH ran through the crowd as they turned
to look at Melanie. Then, at a nod from the
Mayor, the chief of police suddenly relaxed
his grip on the small boy before him. "Son, you've
proved yourself," he said gruffly. "There'll be no more
questions after this. Or threats either. But we had to
be sure, you know."

Maximin's eyes were doubtful. "You mean. . . ."

"He means we all believe now," said Mayor Peytard
kindly. Then, glancing at Melanie: "Come here, my
dear. There's no need to look so frightened."

Timid and not too sure of herself, Melanie obeyed.
But in just a few minutes her heart was at rest. The
Mayor, the chief of police, the various important peo-
ple from Corps, all were now kindness itself. She and
Maximin were not to be taken to jail. Instead, they

were to join with all these new friends in prayers and hymns to Our Lady as they made their way back home.

"If only Father Mélin doesn't get cross with us and believes, too!" thought the little girl, recalling that within twenty-four hours they were to be questioned again by the parish priest of Corps.

But there was no need to worry about this. The next day, when Father Mélin accompanied the children to the place of the apparition, he did not scold or threaten. Nor did he seem displeased because they had failed to follow the advice given by the parish priest of La Salette and had waited more than a week before telling him about their great adventure. Instead, he was gentleness itself—encouraging, suggesting and carefully avoiding any mention of the secrets which Our Lady had confided to her little friends. However, his examination was nonetheless complete for all that, and it was several hours before it was over.

"Father, you do believe Our Lady came, don't you?" asked Maximin eagerly, as they finally started down the mountainside. "You don't think we're lying?"

The priest smiled. "No, son, I believe you and Melanie have told me the truth. There's just one thing—"

"What, Father?"

"See this jar I'm carrying?"

The children nodded. "Yes, you put some water in there from the miraculous spring."

"That's right. Well, I'm taking this water to a very sick woman in my parish. I'm going to have her drink a little of it each day for nine days, and pray to Our Lady for a cure. If that happens—ah, there won't be one doubt left in my mind that the Blessed Virgin did show herself to you."

On October 6, the last day of the novena, Father Mélin was beside himself with joy and wonder. Madame Aglot, the sick woman in question, had arrived at the rectory to report herself entirely free from the aches and pains which had bothered her for years! Even more. Maximin's father, after a visit to the holy mountain, was telling everyone that he was cured of his asthma. Nothing would do now but that he make his confession and receive Holy Communion as soon as possible.

"And this is only the beginning," reflected Father Mélin. "Even the Bishop will probably agree to that."

But the Most Reverend Philibert de Bruillard, the eighty-one-year-old Bishop of Grenoble (in whose diocese Corps and La Salette were situated), was a cautious man, and he refused to commit himself. Perhaps the Blessed Virgin had appeared to Melanie and Maximin, perhaps not. In any case, there must be a careful investigation of the whole affair. And for the time being, no priest was to associate himself officially with any pilgrimages to the holy mountain. Or with public prayers there either. As for old Father Perrin at La Salette, whose health was failing and who had already announced a belief in the apparition from

"YOU DON'T THINK WE'RE LYING, FATHER?"

the pulpit—well, it was probably best to replace him with a younger priest who was not quite so credulous.

"After all, if this affair should turn out to be a mistake on the children's part, we'd be the laughing-stock of all France," he declared bluntly. "No, we must study, watch and wait. Above all, we must pray."

However, the Bishop could not help but be impressed as news of fresh wonders at the site of the apparition began to pour in. What was more, certain learned priests had already begun to make a study of the children's story, and they were all agreed on one point: La Salette, Corps and other neighboring communities were undergoing a remarkable spiritual change. A few months ago only a handful of people had bothered to go to Mass on Sundays, or to receive the Sacraments. The men and boys were especially lax. Why, they were actually ashamed to be seen on their knees! But now the churches were crowded at all hours, even on week days.

"Take the case of Corps, Your Lordship," reported one priest. "Father Mélin's been pastor there for five years, and he knows just about every one of his thirteen hundred parishioners. Last Easter—well, guess how many men approached the Sacraments?"

The Bishop hesitated. "Two hundred, Father?"

"*Two hundred?* Your Lordship, there were scarcely thirty! And most of these came at odd hours when they wouldn't be seen or made fun of for their piety. But now Father Mélin says there are dozens of people going to confession, openly, every day. Even more. A good many men and women won't work on Sundays as they used to. And there isn't nearly as much cursing or swearing as in the past."

The Bishop listened attentively. How wonderful if the Blessed Virgin had actually appeared to Melanie Mathieu and Maximin Giraud! Why, such a miracle in the parish of La Salette could mean the conversion of the whole countryside, perhaps even of all France! People everywhere would begin to see earthly life in its true light. They would understand as never before that it is but a preparation for eternal life in heaven. Gradually they would realize that money, worldly goods and pleasures are of small importance. The main thing is to know, love and serve God and help others to do the same.

"Still, all I can do just now is to be prudent about the whole affair," he decided. "If Our Lady did show herself to the children, if she does want a shrine built at La Salette, she'll see that we have the needed proof."

The priests of the diocese agreed that the Bishop was acting wisely. Accordingly, when six hundred citizens of Corps decided to make a pilgrimage to the place of the apparition on November 17, Father Mélin did not accompany them. Neither did Father Louis Joseph Perrin, the new pastor of La Salette. Everything must be planned by the people themselves, declared the two priests, including the choice of prayers and hymns to be offered along the way.

Of all the people living in Corps, none was more anxious to make the pilgrimage than Marie Laurent, wife of the local baker. "If I could just go along, too!" she told her husband Francis. "Surely Our Lady would cure me if I prayed with the others on the holy mountain?"

A pang shot through the heart of Francis Laurent. His wife had been crippled with rheumatism for twenty-two years. For almost eight years she had had to stay in bed, unable to feed herself or to sit up without assistance. Now that winter was coming on, her pains were even more severe than usual.

"My dear, I'm afraid that's impossible," he said kindly. "You know it's five miles from here to La Salette, besides the long climb up the mountain. The trip would be far too much for you, even in a wagon. And if it should rain or snow—"

Marie Laurent sighed. What Francis said was only too true. She would suffer tortures from being jolted about in a wagon over the rough country roads. And of course there was no way to reach the actual site of the apparition unless someone carried her up the mountain on a stretcher.

"I guess you're right," she admitted sadly. "I'd only be a nuisance to everyone." Then, after a moment: "But promise me one thing."

"What?"

"That you'll pray very hard to Our Lady during the time of the pilgrimage. You know, she could cure me even here at home."

The baker hesitated, not wanting to hurt his wife's feelings yet fearful she was hoping for too much.

"Well—"

"Please, Francis, Our Lady's so good! She knows how hard it is for a wife and mother to be helpless around the house. And wonderful things are going on these days at La Salette. . . ."

Marie's pleading, together with her extreme pain and weakness, were suddenly too much for the kind-hearted baker. "All right, my dear, I'll pray," he said with forced cheerfulness. "What's more, I'll get others to pray, too."

CHAPTER TEN

TRUE TO his word, Francis Laurent lost no time in asking those in charge of the pilgrimage (members of a group known as the Confraternity of Penitents), to make a fervent remembrance of his wife in their prayers when they visited the holy mountain. All agreed to do so, and early in the morning of November 17 the pilgrims left Corps on their arduous march to the place of the apparition.

Ordinarily Marie Laurent would have been resting in bed, but on this occasion she pleaded so earnestly to be allowed to sit in an arm chair by the window that no one had the heart to refuse her.

"And put my crutches beside me," she told the neighbor who came to help her dress. "I may want to use them."

The woman could scarcely believe her ears. "Crutches, Marie? But you haven't had them out in ages! Why, you couldn't even manage to hold them, your hands are so twisted and sore!"

"I know. But bring them anyway," begged the baker's wife. "There's no telling what may happen today."

So the crutches were brought, and from time to time Marie and Francis Laurent prayed fervently together that the Blessed Virgin would work the longed-for miracle. But by mid-afternoon the baker could no longer conceal his true feelings. Long ago the pilgrims had reached the holy mountain. They had remembered Marie in their prayers, and asked the Blessed Virgin to cure her. And since nothing had happened—

"It's all right, dear," said Marie bravely. "I know you've neglected your work all day. Go ahead now and attend to it. But I think I'll pray just a bit longer. . . ."

"Y-you're really not disappointed at the way everything's turned out?"

"Of course not. It's all for the best."

However, once her husband had left the room, Marie Laurent broke into muffled sobs. It had been so long since she had sat up all day, and now every muscle in her body was racked with pain.

"I wanted so much to be cured!" she whimpered. "It . . . it's so hard to be a nuisance to others . . . and I did have such hopes. . . ."

Yet even as discouragement swept over her like a wave, the invalid made a real effort to resign herself

to God's Will. The painful rheumatism, the humili-
ating uselessness of twenty-two years, could be part
of her Purgatory. They could also merit many graces
for sinners. How dreadful, then, to want to be rid of
them!

"Forgive me, dearest Mother!" she murmured. "I
didn't mean what I said." Then, with a last flicker of
childlike hope: "But if it will help others to know and
love you and your Son, please cure me!"

As she prayed, a certain measure of peace filled
Marie's soul. Suffering was so much easier to bear if
one did not try to run away from it! **It** was the strug-
gling against pain that made things hard . . . the
constant urge to order one's life and circumstances
instead of leaving everything to an all-wise God.

"Of course I've always known that," she told herself. "But it's so easy to forget . . . to make plans . . .
to . . . to—dear God! W-what is it? What's happen-
ing to me?"

There was good reason to ask the question, for
suddenly Marie Laurent found herself rising from
the arm chair—her crippled limbs tingling with
unexpected strength, her twisted hands relaxed and
normal.

"Not . . . not a miracle!" she gasped. "Dearest
Mother, you've not worked a miracle after all!"

Yet when the first shock of amazement was over,
Marie Laurent realized that was just what had happened. She was standing on her own two feet, she who
had not been able to rise unassisted from a chair for

almost eight years! And yes—she could take a step, two steps, three steps. . . .

"Francis!" she burst out. "Francis, I'm cured!" And disregarding the crutches on the floor beside her, she hurried across the room and out to the bakeshop where her husband was hard at work.

Of course Francis Laurent could scarcely believe his eyes. His wife was walking like a normal person! She was no longer suffering the slightest pain! She could move about as freely as himself!

"Dear God!" was all he could say. "Dear God!"

That night, when the six hundred pilgrims returned to Corps, no one could talk about anything except the miracle at the baker's house. And when it became known that it had occurred at the very time when the members of the Confraternity of Penitents were reciting their Office at the site of the apparition, excitement was at fever pitch.

"It's proof that the mountain is really a holy spot!" exclaimed the leader of the Confraternity. "Our Lady wants to be honored there."

"Yes, La Salette's going to be one of the most famous places in Europe."

"We'll have to have another pilgrimage."

"When?"

"Why, as soon as possible, of course."

"That's right. Before winter sets in and the weather gets too bad."

So plans were immediately made for a second pilgrimage. However, when November 28, the great day, finally arrived, it was decided that Marie Laurent ought not to take part. A heavy snow was falling, and already there were drifts three to four feet deep along the road to La Salette.

"But I *want* to go!" pleaded the baker's wife. "I'm cured now. I can walk through the snow like anyone else. And I don't mind the cold, really!"

Francis Laurent shook his head. Heaven had undoubtedly worked a miracle for Marie, but what was the point in taking unnecessary risks? Even a man in perfect health would find it hard to walk six miles in the present storm, then repeat the performance.

"No, my dear, it's far better that you stay at home today," he said firmly. "I'll make the pilgrimage for both of us."

Regretfully Marie let herself be persuaded. Yet nothing would do but that she at least go to watch the pilgrims assemble before the parish church. And what a sight met her eyes when she finally arrived! More than fifteen hundred people were on hand, including Maximin and several nuns. There was also an invalid woman on a stretcher. Despite the falling snow and a bitter wind, all were devoutly reciting the Rosary.

Marie looked sympathetically at the sick woman, a victim of dropsy. What faith she must have, and those who had brought her, to be out in such weather! Surely Our Lady would cure her, too?

"I must pray for that," she told herself silently. "I must pray very hard."

CHAPTER ELEVEN

MARIE DID pray fervently all day for that intention. But her heart sank when she went to the outskirts of Corps in the late afternoon to watch the return of the pilgrims. Plodding through the snow in the frosty twilight, footsore and weary, yet still praying and singing in honor of Our Lady, were the fifteen hundred men and women who had set out so bravely that morning for the holy mountain. But there was also a little group, walking more slowly than the rest, carrying a stretcher.

"The poor woman wasn't cured after all!" was the immediate decision of the baker's wife. "Oh, what a pity!"

When the procession had come abreast of her, she silently took a place in the ranks and joined in prayer with the others. But what was her astonishment, when the pilgrims finally disbanded before the parish church, to discover that everyone was in high spirits. The sick woman whom she had seen that morning had been totally cured while kneeling beside the miraculous spring! She had walked all the way home with the others!

"Yes, Our Lady's blessed this pilgrimage, too!" cried Francis Laurent, hurrying to his wife's side. "My dear, I'll never forget this day as long as I live!"

Marie stared. "But I don't understand! Those men over there now, the ones with the stretcher—"

The baker smiled. "Oh, that's something else. Come along, and I'll tell you all about it."

Soon the whole story was out. The sick woman's husband and son had carried her all the way to the holy mountain, forced at times to lift the stretcher to their shoulders because of the enormous snowdrifts. Then, when the Confraternity of Penitents had finished their Office, and as the woman was kneeling beside the miraculous spring, she had uttered a joyful cry. The dropsy from which she had been suffering for so many years had suddenly disappeared! She no longer had the slightest pain or discomfort.

"You can imagine how we all felt about that," declared the baker excitedly. "Why, it seemed as though the Blessed Virgin were actually with us, and that we'd see her at any time!"

Marie nodded. "But the stretcher, Francis! If the woman was really cured. . . ."

"I'm coming to that, my dear. You see, as soon as she knew she was healed, the woman wanted to make some kind of offering to Our Lady. So she took off a gold chain and cross she was wearing and hung them on Maximin's cross."

"*Maximin's cross?* What's that?"

"Just a plain wooden affair the boy set up last month after his father was cured of asthma. But—well, what do you think happened when we were ready to come home?"

"What?"

"One of the men decided to put the woman's trinkets in his pocket. He said it wasn't safe to leave anything valuable on the mountain, and that he'd give the cross and chain to Father Mélin here in Corps."

Marie hesitated. "I suppose that was the wise thing to do. After all, there are thieves in these parts."

"No, no!" cried the baker in horrified tones. "That's what a lot of us thought, too—but only because we didn't have faith."

"Faith! Why, what do you mean?"

"Marie, if Our Lady can work miracles on the mountain, she can make people respect the place, too. Anyway, it wasn't long before this man I'm telling you about had slipped in the snow and fallen into a deep hole. When we finally got him out, we found he'd broken his leg."

Marie's eyes widened with astonishment. "So *he* was the one they were carrying—on the sick woman's stretcher?"

SHE WOULD MAKE AN OFFERING TO OUR LADY.

"That's right. Of course the poor soul meant well enough, but his case certainly taught everyone a good lesson. Only a fool would try to steal anything from the holy mountain now."

True enough. The story of the man who had not believed Our Lady could look after the gifts left in her honor created as much of a stir as though it had concerned a miracle, too. Despite the snow and bitter cold, hundreds of new pilgrims flocked to La Salette, and on December 8 a third pilgrimage was arranged by the Confraternity of Penitents. On this occasion Melanie erected a wooden cross of her own on the site of the apparition, similar to Maximin's, in gratitude for the wonderful grace of having been able to see and speak with the Mother of God on September 19.

Naturally the aged Bishop of Grenoble was kept informed of all that was going on, and his heart filled with gratitude at the news of the great spiritual change that was taking place in the neighborhood of La Salette—the return of hundreds to the Sacraments, the decrease in blasphemy and swearing, the devout way in which Sunday was now being kept by town and countryfolk alike. But he was worried, too. What was to be done about the children who claimed to have seen the Blessed Virgin? On November 24 he had authorized the Sisters of Providence in Corps to receive Maximin as a pupil in their school. But, though winter had long ago set in, Melanie was still at Ablandin's working for Baptiste Pra.

"That little girl should have the chance for an education, too," he told his assistant. "After all, not to be able to read or write at fourteen years of age. . . ."

"Melanie's fifteen now, Your Lordship," put in the assistant respectfully. "She had a birthday on November 7. But even worse than not being able to read or write is the fact that she's quite ignorant of the Catechism and so hasn't been allowed to make her First Communion."

The Bishop nodded thoughtfully. Since early childhood, according to the reports on his desk, Melanie Mathieu had been forced to work as a shepherdess in out-of-the-way places without the chance to go to Mass regularly, let alone to learn the truths of religion. Such was the plight of many a poor youngster in France. But surely this was especially regrettable for one to whom Our Lady had appeared. (Or was *supposed* to have appeared), for until an official inquiry had definitely proved the point the Bishop would not admit, even to himself, that anything extraordinary had taken place in his diocese on September 19.

"Perhaps we'd better arrange for Melanie to go to the Sisters' school in Corps, too," he said finally. "Right after Christmas. Then, if all goes well, she and Maximin will be able to make their First Communion this coming summer."

"Splendid, Your Lordship!" exclaimed the assistant. "I'm sure that will please both the children and their parents."

CHAPTER TWELVE

THE CHILDREN'S parents were pleased with the Bishop's arrangements, especially Peter and Julia Mathieu. Of course their little girl would no longer be a wage-earner, which would be a hardship for the whole family, but she would not be an expense either. She would spend all her time at the Sisters' convent, where she would actually learn to read and write—something few young shepherds in the neighborhood could do.

"Child, you *are* lucky," they told her. "Why, we could never have afforded to send you to the Sisters' school!"

"I know," said Melanie eagerly. "It's just wonderful that I can go."

But only a few days had passed when there began to be many difficulties for Peter Mathieu's young daughter. No matter how hard she studied, she always received poor marks—and in a class of much younger children, too. Maximin also was very slow at books. Like Melanie, he did not have the knack of memorizing, and frequently Mother Saint Thecla, the superior of the convent, was at her wits' end.

"Those children will never make their First Communion this year," she told Father Mélin, the parish priest of Corps. "Why, they can't even learn simple prayers like the Acts of Faith, Hope and Charity!"

The pastor smiled. "Well, Mother, this new life's a bit hard for them," he said reasonably. "They've been accustomed to being outdoors, you know, not cooped up in a classroom. I wouldn't worry too much."

But Mother Saint Thecla did worry. Melanie was so backward and shy, Maximin so lively and mischievous! And it was easy to see why some people still refused to believe Our Lady had appeared on the holy mountain, despite the many wonders which had taken place there. For the children were so ordinary! And when important visitors came to see them and to ask them questions, they were sometimes abrupt to the point of rudeness in their answers—especially if it was a matter of telling their secrets.

"What's going to become of those two?" the good nun often wondered. "And what *are* their secrets?"

But neither Mother Saint Thecla nor anyone else at the convent could get the children to give the slightest hint. Were the secrets good? Maybe. Were they bad? Maybe. Had they to do with the future of France? The world in general? With war or peace? Maybe.

"Those two wouldn't confide in the Pope himself," was the general conclusion.

However, there were other things for the Sisters to worry about. At Christmas time of 1846, as the children had insisted Our Lady had forewarned, the supply of potatoes gave out—not only in the neighborhood of Corps and La Salette, but throughout all France. Then in January word came that things were not much better in other countries either, particularly in Ireland. And because of the potato shortage and the high price of other food, many families were in danger of starvation.

"It's a punishment for our sins," repentant Christians told one another all over Europe. "We haven't been keeping Sunday as we should. We never fasted in Lent or on the Ember Days. Now we're going to have to do penance, just as Our Lady warned those French children."

"Yes, and not only by going hungry. Remember what she said about a plague? Disease always follows a famine. Just wait and see."

True enough. By the time the spring of 1847 had arrived, hundreds of people in Europe were falling victim to the cholera. And in Corps itself, several children had died of a disease no doctor could name.

"Our Lady said the wheat crop would fail, too," one terrified person reminded another. "And the grapes and walnuts. Dear God, what are we going to do?"

Confused and fearful, thousands of new pilgrims took advantage of the fine spring weather to come to the holy mountain in a spirit of prayer and reparation. In June the Stations of the Cross were erected along the path which Our Lady had followed when she had appeared to the children, and soon plans were being made to celebrate the first anniversary of that wonderful day.

True, as yet the Bishop had not publicly declared his belief in the apparition, but that was because he did not want to play into the hands of the enemies of the Church. Recently he had appointed two learned priests from Grenoble, Fathers Rousselot and Orcel, to make a thorough study of the whole affair, including the many cures alleged to have taken place through Our Lady's intercession. Until their final report came in, there would be no statement for or against the apparition. However, the Bishop did relent on one score. On September 19, 1847, he said, the priests of his diocese might take part in a public pilgrimage to the holy mountain. They might also preach there, and offer the Holy Sacrifice.

Father Mélin, the parish priest of Corps, was overjoyed at the news of the unexpected permissions. What a great day the first anniversary was going to be now!

"We'll build a double altar on the mountain," he told Father Louis Joseph Perrin, who, several months ago, had taken the place of the aged pastor of La Salette. "That way, two Masses can be said at once."

"Yes," agreed the younger priest. "But let's make some kind of a shelter, too—a little oratory or chapel. It might rain, you know. Or even snow."

Soon priests and people were busy preparing for the anniversary. But three days beforehand it was evident that they had not done enough. Apparently the whole of France was pouring into Corps, La Salette and other neighboring towns. The inns were completely filled. All space in private homes was gone. Even the barns were housing pilgrims. And for miles around, every available priest was busy hearing confessions.

"There'll be at least ten thousand people going to Holy Communion on the nineteenth," Father Mélin realized in amazement. "God be praised!"

Then late in the afternoon of Saturday, September 18, the good pastor's heart sank. An icy rain had begun to fall, and soon the narrow mountain roads were nothing but rivers of mud. A high wind had sprung up, too, so that umbrellas were well-nigh useless. And yet the crowds kept coming into Corps on their way to La Salette, hundreds and hundreds of them—by fashionable carriage, lumbering farm wagon, on foot—not to mention countless invalids on stretchers.

"What's going to become of all these poor people, particularly the sick?" was the question on everyone's lips. "Once it gets dark, they'll never find their way safely up the mountain. And even if they do, there's no shelter there except the little chapel."

In La Salette, Father Perrin was as worried as anyone else. "The Devil's trying to ruin everything," he reflected soberly. "It'll probably get much worse than this."

True enough. As night came on the storm did get worse, with thunder and lightning and winds of hurricane force. But still the pilgrims kept pouring into La Salette, singing and praying as they pushed on toward their goal. What did it matter that they were soaked to the skin—tired, hungry and cold? That they kept slipping in the mud, falling over stones? That over and over again, lost in the inky blackness, they found themselves on the brink of a dangerous precipice or confronted by a swollen mountain stream? They had come to do penance for their sins, to implore Our Lady's help against famine and disease, to seek a bodily or spiritual cure. There must be no turning back now.

CHAPTER THIRTEEN

A ROUND MIDNIGHT the rain ceased, but a heavy fog took its place. The wooden chapel erected near the site of the apparition was crowded to capacity. Here some eighty priests took turns in reciting the Rosary and other prayers in honor of the Blessed Virgin, while outside, huddled together in the chill darkness, two thousand pilgrims joined in as best they could. Then, at half-past two in the morning, Father Louis Joseph Perrin, pastor of La Salette, blessed the chapel, after which he commenced the Holy Sacrifice of the Mass on one side of the double altar, while his brother, Father James Michael Perrin, did the same on the other. This procedure was repeated several times, with the Communion rail constantly crowded.

At dawn the fog still persisted, but at frequent intervals a slight breeze caused it to lift for a minute or so. Then all eyes turned toward the darkened valley, where miles of flickering torches announced the progress of still more pilgrims. Occasionally the wind carried their voices, too, raised in prayer and hymns in honor of the Blessed Virgin. Then, about ten o'clock, the fog suddenly rolled away. The sun burst forth in all its glory, whereupon an amazing sight greeted the eye. The two thousand men and women who had spent the night on the rain-soaked mountain had been joined by twenty thousand more! And at least twice this number were moving along the muddy road below!

"More than forty thousand people!" exclaimed the pastor of Corps in awestruck tones. "Why, I can scarcely believe my eyes!"

But soon the number was on the increase. Indeed, shortly before noon the crowds were so dense about the little chapel, the danger of suffocation so great, that it was deemed necessary to alter the plan for the celebration of Holy Mass. Instead, there would be a sermon by a young priest named Father Sibillat.

Eagerly the immense crowd settled itself to hear the story of Our Lady of La Salette. However, the speaker's words reached only a fraction of his audience. An hour or so later, a sermon by Father John Baptist Gerin, rector of the Cathedral in Grenoble, fared little better, and finally it was decided that the public recitation of the Rosary would be more practical. Thus, until two o'clock or so, priests and people joined in this familiar prayer to Our Lady, together with favorite hymns in her honor.

"What a wonderful day!" thought Father Mélin, thrilling to the echo of thousands of voices rising from the holy mountain. "Why, it's one of the greatest days in my life!"

Melanie and Maximin were as pleased as their parish priest at all the homage being paid the Blessed Virgin. Of course it was hard to be pushed about so much, to have to answer the hundreds of questions put to them by eager pilgrims. But they did their best to cooperate, even to the point of repeating, several times, the whole story of what had happened a year ago in this very place.

However, some of the Sisters from the convent in Corps grew slightly anxious as they watched and listened. In their opinion, so much attention was not good for the children's characters. It would be the easiest thing in the world for the young shepherds to become proud and self-willed because of all the respect being paid to them. For the pilgrims were actually hanging on their every word! They were even asking for advice on various problems, and bringing religious articles for the children to touch as though they were saints!

"No, Sisters, I don't think there's any danger the little ones will get puffed up about all this," Mother Saint Thecla reassured her companions. "After all,

THE VALLEY WAS FILLED WITH PILGRIMS.

how could they think much of themselves when they
have such poor records at school?"

Actually the same thought had occurred to Mother
Saint Thecla when the children had first been given
into her care, and so she had seen to it that Melanie
and Maximin received exactly the same treatment
as their classmates. There were no special favors or
permissions. The apparition of Our Lady was seldom
mentioned, save when particularly devout pilgrims
came to see the children and to ask them questions.
Then, to the good nun's relief, the latter seemed only
too anxious to escape from their visitors as soon as
possible and to return to their regular work.

"No, I guess pride doesn't have a place in these little ones' hearts," she had reflected from time to time.
"Thank God for that."

A few weeks after the celebration on the mountain came unexpected news. Bishop de Bruillard
announced that Melanie and Maximin were to be
brought to Grenoble. Here they would appear before
an official committee of sixteen priests to answer
questions about the vision of Our Lady which they
claimed to have had. Mother Saint Thecla and
another religious would accompany Melanie. Father
Mélin, the pastor of Corps, would accompany Maximin. Both children were to be at the Bishop's house
on November 15 to tell their respective stories.

Mother Saint Thecla heard the news with mixed
feelings. Of course it was splendid that a thorough
study of Our Lady's apparition was being made. But

neither Melanie nor Maximin had ever been in a large city before, nor had they met Bishop de Bruillard. Perhaps they would be so overcome by the experience that they would make a very poor showing before those sixteen learned priests. Melanie especially would likely be nervous and upset and unable to speak up well. Then, how the enemies of the Church would rejoice! It would be harder than ever to get them to believe that Our Lady had actually given the world an important message.

"Why, I think the experience will be just the thing for the children, Mother," observed one of the Sisters. "After all, it'll be good for their pride if they don't make a favorable impression on the Bishop's committee."

"But—"

"That's right, Mother," put in another religious. "And don't worry. If the Blessed Virgin wants to be honored on the holy mountain, she'll see to it that everything turns out well."

CHAPTER FOURTEEN

O N NOVEMBER 8 the first meeting of the
Bishop's committee took place. On this occasion Fathers Rousselot and Orcel outlined
the careful study of the apparition which they had
been making since the previous July, and their several interviews with the young shepherds. Then they
gave a detailed description of the mountain pasture
where Our Lady was said to have shown herself. The
Bishop and his sixteen advisers listened carefully,
asked questions and made several notes. But it was
on November 15 that things took a really lively turn.
Then it was that Maximin was brought in to tell his
story. And contrary to Mother Saint Thecla's fears,
the boy was not at all excited or embarrassed. In fact,
he was quite at ease, bouncing up and down with

evident relish in the comfortable chair which had been provided for him

"All right," he announced to the sixteen rather startled priests before him. "What is it you want to know, Fathers?"

Bishop de Bruillard suppressed a smile. "Tell us what happened near La Salette last year on September 19," he suggested. "And take your time, Maximin. There's no need to hurry."

The distinguished audience leaned forward eagerly, although some were frowning a bit at the restlessness of their young guest. Ever since this twelve-year-old boy had come into the room he had not been still a minute. Either he had been bouncing up and down in his chair or balancing himself on the arms or back. Surely the Blessed Virgin had never appeared to such a light-headed little rascal! And yet there was something likable about him, too . . . something sincere and refreshing. . . .

Maximin, totally unconcerned at the various impressions he was making, began a matter-of-fact description of all that had taken place in the mountain pasture on September 19, 1846—Our Lady's dress, her tears, her message, the wonderful way she had walked on the tips of the grass blades without bending them, her final disappearance into thin air.

"She gave you a secret, too, didn't she?" prompted the Bishop. "Something very important?"

Suddenly a change came over Maximin. He ceased his fidgeting and became very grave. "Yes, but I can't talk about that," he declared flatly.

The Bishop smiled. "Come, lad, of course you can. These good priests here won't breathe a word of what you say to anyone, and neither will I. Now, what's this marvelous secret?"

Maximin shook his head. "I can't tell you."

"But I'm your Bishop, son! Surely you ought to obey me when I ask you to do something?"

"No, it's better to obey the Blessed Virgin. And she said not to tell anyone." Suddenly one of the priests in the audience rose to his feet. "The Blessed Virgin!" he burst out impatiently. "I thought you said you didn't know who the lady was when you first saw her. Or Melanie either."

Maximin shrugged. "We didn't, Father. But afterwards different people said that's who it must have been."

"What people?"

"Madame Pra and her mother. And old Father Perrin, who used to be at La Salette. And lots of others."

"Nonsense! It was just some strange woman pretending to be the Blessed Virgin."

Once again Maximin shook his head vigorously. "Oh, no, Father. An ordinary woman couldn't walk on top of the grass blades without bending them. Or have so much brightness about her that she didn't cast a shadow, even though the sun was shining."

Suddenly another priest rose to his feet. "Maximin, maybe the lady was an evil spirit," he suggested thoughtfully. "The Devil and his angels can take to themselves all kinds of forms, you know, and deceive even the holiest people."

The boy's eyes darkened. "An evil spirit wouldn't be sad because people curse and swear, Father. And miss Mass on Sundays."

"No. But—well, maybe you dreamed this whole business about the beautiful lady. You did say you took a nap on the mountain, you know."

"Then what about the miraculous spring? That's no dream. Or the cures that have taken place there."

Fathers Rousselot and Orcel exchanged satisfied glances. Maximin was certainly conducting himself very creditably. Nothing seemed to disturb him, not even the trickiest questions. Now, if only Melanie could do as well. . . .

There was not long to wait. The next day, in company with Mother Saint Thecla, Melanie appeared before the Bishop's committee. A bit pale, and with downcast eyes, she meekly took her place in the arm chair provided for her—a distinct contrast to the lively witness of the day before. But in just a few minutes she, too, was quite at ease. Each question put to her was answered with politeness and dispatch. Only when it was a matter of discussing her secret did she seem at all disturbed. Then, like Maximin, she shook her head stubbornly.

"No, I can't talk about that," was her only comment. Naturally the committee could not help but be impressed by the artless sincerity of the two young shepherds. Neither had heard the other speak. The questions and objections of those present were new to each, yet the answers were wonderfully alike. The only puzzling thing was that the youngsters did not seem to be especially holy or interested in spiritual things. For instance, twelve-year-old Maximin had not learned enough Latin to be able to serve Mass properly, although he had been coached regularly for several months. Sixteen-year-old Melanie was still unable to recite the Acts of Faith, Hope and Charity, although she was required to study them twice a day.

Finally Mother Saint Thecla ventured an opinion. "Maybe it's only the simple and innocent who can teach the modern world anything," she said.

The Bishop and his advisers were silent. How true that God had no need of any creature to help Him with His work! Indeed, through the ages it had often been the least likely souls whom He had used to proclaim His glory. The young boy David, for instance, who had slain the giant Goliath when all the odds were against it; Peter the Apostle, who had become Head of His Church after denying Christ three times; and right now, in the little French village of Ars, the saintly Father John Marie Vianney, whose superiors had once declared he was too stupid to have a vocation to the priesthood.

And on September 19, the second anniversary of the apparition, at least fifteen thousand people were on hand for a colorful celebration on the holy mountain.

Naturally most of the pilgrims were anxious to see and speak with the children and to learn what plans were being made for them. Surely these two privileged souls weren't going to be boarders much longer at the Sisters' school in Corps? Why, Melanie was almost seventeen! And Maximin was also growing up. What was to be done about their future?

Rumors of all sorts abounded, and one persisted more than the rest. Melanie planned to join the Sisters of Providence, her teachers, whose Motherhouse was at Corenc. Maximin had hopes of becoming a priest, and so would soon be entering the Minor Seminary near Grenoble.

"Is this true, Father?" curious strangers asked the pastor of Corps.

Father Mélin hesitated. "Well, it would be nice if the children had vocations to God's service," he admitted guardedly. Then, with a smile: "But I'm afraid nothing definite has been decided yet."

However, when Maximin's father died on February 24, 1849, Father Mélin felt that it was high time something definite was decided. For the moment Louis Templier, Maximin's uncle, was acting as the boy's guardian. He was a good enough man, but woefully ignorant, and gossip had it that he was seriously considering the idea of taking his young nephew on a tour of France and charging people for the privilege of seeing and speaking with him. Peter Mathieu, Melanie's father, had agreed that this would be an easy way to make a living. He would like to enter into a partnership with Louis and bring Melanie along, too.

"Dear God, we just can't let such scandalous things happen!" Father Mélin thought with dismay. "If Melanie wants to join the Sisters of Providence, she ought to go to Corenc as soon as possible. But as for getting Maximin out of harm's way by putting him in the Minor Seminary—well, he's never been a scholar. And how he can hope to follow the regular course of studies and become a priest is beyond me."

Bishop de Bruillard had a suggestion. "Why couldn't you help the boy, Father?" he asked one day.

Father Mélin looked up in astonishment. "*I,* Your Lordship? But how? I've thought and thought. . . ."

"Maximin's poor in Latin, isn't he?"

"Terribly poor, Your Lordship. That's just what bothers me. He'd never be able to keep up with the others at the Minor Seminary."

"Then why not coach him a little? Of course he ought to stay on at the Sisters' school. But after classes there, it wouldn't do any harm if he came to the rectory for special work with you."

Father Mélin readily agreed to give the Bishop's plan a trial. However, after some months he found himself deeply discouraged. Surely Maximin would never succeed as a seminarian! All his life the boy had shied away from study. Now that he was fourteen, he was less interested in it than ever. Even worse. Of late he had developed an alarming streak of independence and on several occasions had slipped away from the Sisters' school to roam the countryside or to play with his friends in Corps. Once he had even gone as far as Ablandins and stayed with Baptiste Pra for three days and nights.

"Nothing we say or do seems to make any difference," reported Mother Saint Thecla tearfully. "Oh, Father, what's going to become of the poor little lad?"

"The poor little lad!" burst out Father Mélin, now thoroughly exasperated. "Who knows? In my opinion he deserves a good thrashing, that's what. After all we've done for him, he might at least show some consideration for our feelings."

However, no one could remain angry with Maximin. "I just don't seem able to stay long in one place," was the excuse he always offered. And with such wistful charm and affection that everyone was moved into forgiving him for still another time.

Thus, despite frequent lapses from grace, Maximin continued with his Latin lessons at the rectory. But by the fall of 1849, Father Mélin was more doubtful than ever of the boy's vocation to the priesthood. Gradually he had discovered that one reason he was so backward was that he saw no need to study. A person didn't have to know a lot in order to love God and Our Lady, did he?

"I don't see why I can't be a priest right now," announced Maximin one day. "Why, this very minute I know I could preach a really wonderful sermon."

Father Mélin stared in mock astonishment. "You could?"

"Yes. All I'd have to do would be to get up in the pulpit and repeat what Our Lady said three years ago. You know, Father, the part about keeping Sundays holy and not cursing or swearing. 'Do like I do,' I'd say, and everyone would be converted."

The priest suppressed a smile. "So you think a person can become a saint by being disobedient and lazy and careless—like someone I know?"

Maximin shrugged. "Oh, but those are just little faults. If that's all that people did wrong, the world wouldn't be such a bad place."

Father Mélin was reduced to silence. What an impossible boy! A stranger would certainly consider him aggravating beyond words, and filled with outrageous pride. But of course Maximin wasn't proud. He was—well, just himself. A simple, happy-go-lucky youngster with scarcely a prudent thought in his head.

"Son, I wouldn't worry too much about preaching a sermon just now," he said finally. "Or even tomorrow. That great event will probably keep for quite some time."

"WHY CAN'T I BE A PRIEST RIGHT AWAY?"

CHAPTER SIXTEEN

I T WAS in the spring of 1850 that definite steps
were taken concerning the future of the two children. After more than three years at the Sisters'
school in Corps, they were to return home for a little
vacation. In June, when Bishop Dépéry of Gap visited
Corps, they would receive the Sacrament of Confir-
mation. Then, towards the end of September, Melanie
would enter the Sisters of Providence at Corenc and
Maximin the Minor Seminary near Grenoble.

However, some well-to-do laymen from Paris and
Caen, while admitting the wisdom of these plans, had
also made plans of their own. Surely it would do the
children no harm to visit Father John Marie Vianney,
the saintly parish priest of Ars? This was an experience sought after by thousands of people, including
the holiest priests and religious.

"Oh, I'd love a trip like that!" exclaimed Maximin when the suggestion was made to him. And when his would-be benefactors also suggested that perhaps he might like to study for the priesthood with the Marist Fathers in Lyons, rather than at the Minor Seminary near Grenoble, he was even more excited. A trip to the big city of Lyons, too? How wonderful!

Soon arrangements were being made. Maximin's three friends would take him to Grenoble on September 22, three days after the celebration of the fourth anniversary of Our Lady's apparition on the holy mountain. From there the group would go to Lyons and thence to Ars, eighteen miles away. Enlightened by the Holy Spirit, Father Vianney would quickly inform the boy where he would be most likely to succeed in his studies. As for twenty-one-year-old Angelica Giraud, Maximin's stepsister, currently employed as a servant in Grenoble, it might be a good thing for her to come along, too. Undoubtedly Father Vianney would also be able to throw some light on her vocation. Later, when the problems of Maximin and Angelica had been settled, Melanie would have her trip.

Father Mélin was far from pleased when he heard about all this. In fact, he was extremely worried and annoyed. "You know the children aren't permitted to go outside the diocese," he told Maximin's uncle and Melanie's father. "The Bishop made that ruling long ago."

Louis Templier shrugged. So did Peter Mathieu. "There's nothing wrong with visiting a holy man like

Father Vianney," they said. "Everyone knows he's a saint."

"That's not the point. His Lordship wants the children to spend these last few days in the world in peace and quiet. At Lyons and Ars there'd be nothing but excitement, crowds, publicity. No, no, my friends. Such a trip is out of the question."

These words fell on deaf ears, however. De Brayer, Verrier and Thibault, the children's would-be benefactors, were important men. Already they had been very good to the Giraud and Mathieu families. De Brayer had even made a gift of five hundred francs to Melanie's father. Then he was a friend of a man named Bonafous. And everyone knew that Bonafous was intimately connected with the Baron de Richemont, pretender to the throne of France. If the day should come when the Baron was crowned king, there would certainly be many more privileges for the children and their families through the good offices of the Baron's friends.

"We can't afford to listen to Father Mélin when he doesn't understand all this," Louis Templier told Peter Mathieu indignantly. "Why, here's the opportunity of a lifetime for the children!"

"Of course," said Peter. "There's absolutely no reason why they shouldn't go."

So on September 22, fifteen-year-old Maximin found himself embarked on a glorious adventure. With his uncle's wholehearted permission, he was on his way to see a saint. And traveling with him were three men who were not only kind and sympathetic but possessed of considerable means as well.

"How lucky I am!" the boy told himself. "And Angelica, too!"

However, when the group arrived in Grenoble, Maximin caused his friends no little concern by suggesting a visit with Father John Baptist Gerin, the rector of the Cathedral. He had not seen this good priest in some time, and, in his innocence, was eager to tell him all about the present trip.

De Brayer, Verrier and Thibault looked at one another anxiously. They were good men, and had Maximin's welfare much at heart, but they had no wish to meet anyone from the Cathedral just now. Well they knew that the Bishop and his advisers were greatly averse to allowing either of the children to leave the diocese. Of course the official inquiry concerning the apparition was not yet complete, and from time to time the youngsters were needed for questioning. Still, this seemed no reason to forego the great spiritual good that always followed a visit with the parish priest of Ars—

"Son, why don't we go to see Father Gerin on our way back?" they suggested. "There'd be time then for a really worthwhile visit. But now, when we have to find out about leaving for Lyons. . . ."

"No, I want to see Father Gerin right away," said Maximin stubbornly. "He's a friend of mine."

Fearful of a scene, the three men reluctantly took Maximin to the Cathedral and promised to call for him later. But on their return, their worst fears were realized. Father Gerin had lost no time in informing Bishop de Bruillard of Maximin's approaching visit to Ars, also of the half-formed plan to enroll him as a student at the Marist house in Lyons. The result? The Bishop had promptly forbidden the lad to leave Grenoble. He was to go at once to a house of the Brothers of the Christian Schools and remain there until the opening of the Minor Seminary.

Deep gloom descended upon the would-be benefactors. What was to be done now? "Well, Maximin, you'll have to obey His Lordship," they decided finally. "After all, he is your Bishop."

The boy nodded slowly. "Y-yes," he admitted, in a very small voice. "I know."

For a moment the three men looked at one another. Poor Maximin! He was taking everything very hard, even harder than they were. Then suddenly de Brayer had a comforting idea. Of course Maximin must go at once to the Christian Brothers' house, as the Bishop had ordered, but perhaps the final farewell could be postponed for a little while? Perhaps they could all have supper together before the scheduled departure for Lyons?

Maximin's spirits immediately rose. And when matters were arranged with the superior at the Christian Brothers' house, he settled down quite cheerfully in his new quarters. He was cheerful, too, when his three friends came that night to take him to supper.

But afterwards, when they attempted to return him to his new home, his mood suddenly changed.

"No, I'm not staying with those Brothers," he declared, bursting into tears. "I . . . I hate it there!"

The men stared in amazement. "But you have to, Maximin! The Bishop said. . . ."

"I don't care what he said! You promised I could go with you to Lyons. And to Ars, too. And now. . . ."

At once there was a hasty effort to comfort the boy and to get him to listen to reason. All to no avail. Maximin was heartbroken. He would rather spend the night in the street than return to the Brothers' house.

"You promised I could see Father Vianney!" he kept sobbing. "You promised!"

At their wits' end, the three men held a whispered consultation. Certainly a fifteen-year-old country boy couldn't be left by himself in a strange city. And since darkness had now fallen and it was almost time to be off for Lyons. . . .

"We'll have to take the lad with us after all," they decided uneasily. "There's nothing else to do."

CHAPTER SEVENTEEN

O F COURSE Bishop de Bruillard was distressed when he heard what had happened. Maximin's three friends might be well-meaning enough, but there was good reason to believe, in the light of their association with Baron de Richemont, that they had hopes of using the boy for political ends.

"They think his famous secret concerns the Baron's chances to become King Louis the Seventeenth," the Bishop told Father Gerin. "And they're determined to get it from him at all costs. Dear God, once they start confusing the boy, and mixing religion with politics. . . ."

Father Gerin nodded. "That's just what our enemies would like, Your Lordship—the chance to say that La Salette is only a scheme to further the ends of some political group. What *are* we going to do?"

The Bishop shook his head gloomily. "I don't know, Father. Prayer's the only way out, I guess."

So the two set themselves to praying as never before, hoping that Maximin, in his innocence, would not allow himself to be used for any unseemly purpose, and making what plans they could for the boy's future. However, only a few days later there was fresh cause for alarm. De Brayer, Verrier and Thibault had not brought Maximin back to Corps, or even to Grenoble. Now the word was that they had succeeded in arranging an interview with Father John Marie Vianney, and in his presence the boy had retracted his entire story of what had happened at La Salette! As a result, the sixty-four-year-old priest was no longer blessing pictures or medals of the apparition. Everything was a lie, he said, and both children impostors.

The Bishop could scarcely believe his ears. "It can't be!" he kept exclaiming. "There's been some horrible mistake!"

But certain friends who passed through Grenoble on their way home from Ars (for more than twenty years, because of the presence of Father Vianney, one of the most famous pilgrimage spots in France), confirmed the story. Maximin had spoken with Father Vianney twice and admitted that nothing miraculous had occurred on the holy mountain four years ago. He and Melanie had made up everything.

"Well, I still don't believe it," said the Bishop emphatically. "Not until I've seen and talked to Maximin myself."

But where was the boy? No one seemed to know. Then, to everyone's relief, word came that he was staying at a boarding house near Lyons in the care of Father Bez, a priest whom the Bishop knew and trusted. (His three friends had long since withdrawn from their association with him, confused and disappointed over what had happened at Ars.)

"Have Maximin come to Grenoble at once," the Bishop ordered Father Gerin. "We've simply got to get to the bottom of this whole affair."

The latter readily agreed: "Yes, Your Lordship. But what about the Minor Seminary? Are you still planning to enroll the boy there?"

"Of course, Father. I have lots of confidence in him even yet."

So presently Maximin was back in Grenoble. But instead of being fearful and crestfallen when brought before the Bishop for questioning, he was his usual carefree self. In fact, when asked to explain what had happened at Ars, he began to laugh heartily.

"Not much," he said.

"Not much!" exclaimed the Bishop, stiffening with annoyance. "What do you mean, lad? You denied everything, didn't you? You confessed that you and Melanie had never seen a beautiful lady. . . ."

"Oh, no, Your Lordship. I never said that."

"What did you say then?"

Maximin hesitated. Never before had he seen the Bishop so disturbed. "I . . . I guess maybe I'd better start at the beginning," he suggested.

The Bishop nodded curtly. "That would be the best thing This whole scandalous business demands a thorough explanation."

So, in a somewhat subdued frame of mind, Maximin began his story—describing how his three guides had taken Angelica and himself to Lyons, thence to Ars, where they had arrived on the night of September 24. They had gone at once to set Father Vianney, but he was busy hearing confessions in the parish church. Father Raymond, his assistant, had spoken to them instead. And none too cordially.

"I didn't like him at all, Your Lordship," declared the boy scowling, "especially when he said I had lied about everything at La Salette and that Father Vianney, being a saint, would soon find me out."

The Bishop's eyes shot open with astonishment. "Maximin! He didn't say that!"

"He did, too. Father Raymond wasn't a bit nice to me. You know, I think he still has a grudge because of what happened when he visited La Salette."

"What! You'd met this priest before?"

"Yes, a couple of years ago when he made a pilgrimage to the holy mountain. At that time he wasn't allowed to say Mass in the parish church because he hadn't brought along the necessary papers to show Father Perrin who he was. And when he tried to talk to me, I was in a bad mood and wouldn't have anything to do with him."

A dozen questions were on the Bishop's tongue, but he held his peace. "Go on," he said. "What happened next?"

"Well, I got really peeved with Father Raymond, Your Lordship. I said: 'Have it your own way, Father. Tell people I'm a liar and saw nothing on the holy mountain.' Then I walked away."

"So you didn't see Father Vianney that night?"

"No, only the next morning in the sacristy."

"What happened then?"

"I asked him about my vocation, but he didn't seem to have any ideas. All he said was that I ought to go back to my own diocese and do what I was told. That didn't please me, or my friends either, so later in the day I went to see Father Vianney again. This time he was hearing confessions behind the main altar. I went in the confessional when my turn came, although I wasn't planning to go to confession myself, and began to talk to him."

"Yes. And what did he say?"

Frowning slightly, Maximin continued: "Not what I wanted to hear, Your Lordship. Evidently Father Raymond had been telling him, and a lot of other people, too, that the night before I had admitted being a liar and had seen nothing on the holy mountain."

"But you didn't intend those words to be taken seriously!"

"Of course not. But when I found they had been, I got very cross. I said to myself: 'Let's see if this old priest is really a saint and can read my mind.'"

"You weren't rude to Father Vianney!"

"Not exactly. But I guess he knew I didn't care very much for him. He was so deaf, with only a few teeth, and half the time I couldn't understand what he was saying. But I did understand when he told me I must fix up any lies I'd told. I explained I couldn't do that because there were so many, I'd told them so long ago, and it didn't seem worth the trouble to set them straight now."

"What did he say to that?"

"The same as before. I must take back all my lies."

"By 'lies' you meant small falsehoods you'd told as a child?"

"Yes. To my family, the parish priest in Corps, the Sisters at school. . . ."

"You didn't mean anything connected with La Salette?"

"Oh, no! I've never lied about that."

"Still, you let Father Vianney think you did."

"I . . . I suppose so."

"You know you did, lad! In fact, in your thoughts, you had already dared him to read your mind."

Maximin shrugged. "Well, I was still awfully put out over what Father Raymond had said, Your Lordship . . . about Father Vianney's being a saint and able to prove me a liar."

For a moment the Bishop was silent. Gradually things were becoming clear. For some strange reason, known only to God, Father Vianney had failed to understand Maximin and Maximin to understand Father Vianney. And most of the confusion was due to Father Raymond, who had repeated the idle words the boy had spoken upon his arrival in Ars. No

"ALL RIGHT, FATHER. TELL PEOPLE I'M A LIAR. . . ."

wonder the little village was buzzing with the rumor that there had been no heavenly apparition on the holy mountain; that Our Lady of La Salette was only a myth.

"Well, there's not much we can do about anything now," said the Bishop dryly. "The damage is done. We'll just have to hope that things clear up before too long. And as for you. . . ."

Maximin looked up eagerly. "Yes, Your Lordship?"

"I was planning to send you to the Minor Seminary, you know. But now, when you've been so disobedient and thoughtless. . . ."

Suddenly the light faded from Maximin's eyes. Surely the Bishop didn't mean—

"I . . . I'm sorry for everything!" he burst out. "I won't ever disobey you again."

"Ah, I've heard those words before."

"But this time I mean them, Your Lordship! Oh, please don't send me back to Corps! Let me go to the Seminary, like you promised! I want to be a priest so much!"

The Bishop's face was stern. "So, you think a boy with all your faults would make a good priest?"

"I . . . I'd try to be one, Your Lordship. Really and truly!"

Once again the Bishop lapsed into thoughtful silence. Considering Maximin's unstable character, the chances that he would persevere in the arduous studies for the priesthood were very slim. And he certainly deserved no more favors. On the other hand, there might be a miracle of sorts and he would mend his ways.

"Well, son, I don't know. . . ."

By now Maximin was quivering with excitement. "Please, Your Lordship, I'll never give you any more trouble if you'll just let me go to the Seminary! I'll pray, I'll study hard, I'll be polite, I'll do everything I'm told. . . ."

The Bishop permitted himself a slight smile. What an imposing lot of promises! And how unlikely that even one of them would be kept! But after a moment's reflection he found himself setting aside his doubts.

"All right," he said finally. "I'll give you one more chance to prove yourself, Maximin. But if you don't use it to advantage. . . ."

The boy's eyes shone with relief. "Oh, I will, Your Lordship!" he exclaimed fervently. "I will! Just wait and see!"

CHAPTER EIGHTEEN

AS SOON as he had enrolled fifteen-year-old Maximin at the Minor Seminary, Bishop de Bruillard set about mending the damage caused by the boy's trip to Ars. An explanatory letter was sent to Father Vianney, begging him to do his part in putting an end to the story that nothing miraculous had taken place on the holy mountain. Then Fathers Rousselot and Mélin went to Ars in person in a further attempt to set things straight. All to no avail.

"Maximin made a very bad impression on Father Vianney," they informed the Bishop presently. "He just can't bring himself to believe in La Salette any more."

The Bishop groaned. "But surely you explained things to him—how the boy was tired and out-of-sorts the night he spoke to Father Raymond; that he may have told lies about some things but never about the apparition. . . ."

The two priests shook their heads. They had gone into all these matters thoroughly, but still Father Vianney was unconvinced. As for Father Raymond, he seemed to take a peculiar satisfaction in making light of everything connected with La Salette. Whenever he could, he scoffed and warned people against it.

The Bishop's heart sank still farther. Father Raymond was only an assistant at Ars, and not too important, but everyone knew that Father John Marie Vianney, the pastor, was a saint. As soon as it became general knowledge that he had lost faith in La Salette, that he was no longer blessing medals or pictures of the apparition—

"Dear God, what trouble there's going to be!" reflected the Bishop uneasily. "Why, this is just the sort of thing our enemies have been waiting for!"

True enough. Thousands of devout people were shocked and confused when they learned that the parish priest of Ars no longer believed Our Lady had appeared at La Salette. Many who had hoped to visit the holy mountain now changed their plans.

"Those children are impostors," they told one another indignantly. "It took Father Vianney only a few minutes to find that out."

"Yes, the wretches! Let's hope they're well punished for what they've done."

"And to think they kept up their lies for over four years!"

"And fooled even the holiest people!"

"Well, their little game is up now."

"That's right. There'll be no more pilgrimages to La Salette."

But even as tongues wagged, many clients of Our Lady loyally defended the belief in her apparition on the holy mountain. Granted that the pastor of Ars, who was a saint, did not believe the children had enjoyed a heavenly vision—what about the many cures that had taken place at La Salette? And the miraculous spring which had never ceased to flow, summer or winter, since September, 1846?

"There's something wonderful about the place, in spite of everything," they insisted. "Perhaps if Father Vianney went there himself. . . ."

"Nonsense! The spring's the work of the Devil. And the cures, too."

"But the Devil can't work miracles!"

"Of course he can—with God's permission."

"Well, what about the prophecy that the potato crop would fail? The grapes and walnuts and the wheat? Everything's happened just like the children said it would."

"That's the work of the Devil, too."

"No, no! That doesn't make sense."

"Of course it doesn't."

"Our Lady did come to La Salette."

"She did not!"

"She did!"

"She did not!"

"She did!"

As the days passed, the arguments for and against the apparition waxed hotter and hotter, with the Bishop and his advisers having many an anxious conference. What a pity that Maximin had ever gone to Ars! Why couldn't he have listened to reason like Melanie? She, too, had wanted to see the famous little village. In fact, shortly after Maximin's visit, her father had brought her as far as Grenoble. But then, fortunately, the two had decided to obey the Bishop's order not to leave the diocese, and Melanie had gone instead to the Motherhouse of the Sisters of Providence at Corenc. Here she was now established as a postulant and doing very nicely. God willing, she would receive the holy habit in a year's time.

"Let's hope some good comes out of Maximin's disobedience even yet," the pastor of Corps told the Bishop one day. "Stranger things than that have happened through prayer, Your Lordship."

The Bishop nodded. "Of course," he agreed cheerfully. "Real prayer can work miracles."

But by Christmas time of 1850, it was evident that no miracles were in the making. La Salette had become one of the stormiest issues in France, chiefly because the saintly parish priest of Ars had convinced himself that Maximin was an idle, deceitful boy who had lied about seeing Our Lady and now refused to admit his fault. Father Raymond was also adding to the general confusion by advising the thousands of pilgrims who came to Ars to stay away from La Salette. It was a waste of time to go there, he said. Nothing miraculous had ever happened in that out-of-the-way spot and nothing ever would.

Then one day in March, 1851, an exciting letter arrived at the Bishop's house. His Holiness, Pope Pius the Ninth, had heard about the controversy over La Salette and wanted to know the complete story of the apparition, including the famous secrets! Perhaps the children would write these down and send them to him by trusted messenger?

Bishop de Bruillard was encouraged by the Holy Father's interest in La Salette, seeing in it the first actual good to result from the unfortunate incident at Ars. But he was also a little worried. During the past four and one-half years, Melanie and Maximin had steadfastly refused to give the slightest hint as to their respective secrets. Threats, bribes, arguments of all sorts, had proved absolutely fruitless.

"Now what's going to happen?" the Bishop reflected uneasily. "There'll be more gossip than ever if the children refuse to obey the Holy Father. On the other hand, if the Blessed Virgin actually told them not to give the secrets to anyone. . . ."

The Bishop's advisers quickly reached a decision. "Someone must go to see the children at once," they declared. "Someone who can be both firm and gentle, and make them understand the situation."

The Bishop hesitated. By virtue of his position, he was certainly the one to speak to Melanie and Maximin about the Pope's request. But recently he had not been at all well. And since the March days were cold and blustery. . . .

"Father, suppose you go," he suggested to his secretary, Father Auvergne. "Maximin's at the Minor Seminary, you know, and Melanie at the Motherhouse of the Sisters of Providence in Corenc."

The secretary stared. "*I,* Your Lordship?"

"Yes. Explain about my health, and emphasize to the children how important it is that they do what the Holy Father has asked."

"But . . . but I have no influence with the children, Your Lordship! Why, they hardly know me!"

"Perhaps not. But it won't do any harm to go and see them, Father, and to find out what they think about writing down their secrets for the Pope."

As he stood gazing doubtfully at his superior, a pang shot through the heart of Father Auvergne. How tired the Bishop looked! How strained and worn! Why, he seemed even older than his eighty-five years. . . .

"The trouble over the apparition has been too much," he reflected. "Far too much." Then aloud, and with forced cheerfulness:

"Well, Your Lordship, I suppose I *could* go."

The Bishop smiled faintly, sighed and closed his eyes. "Good," he murmured. "And don't lose any time, Father. This whole affair is terribly important. . . ."

CHAPTER NINETEEN

WITH CONSIDERABLE misgivings, Father Auvergne set out to see Maximin at the Minor Seminary.

"Holy Spirit, give me the right words to say!" he pleaded silently. "All this means so much to the Church, and I haven't the slightest idea of how to begin. . . ."

However, when the time for the interview finally arrived, Father Auvergne found himself remarkably composed.

"Maximin, what I'm about to tell you is very important," he announced. "Promise that you won't repeat it to anyone?"

The boy nodded cheerfully. "Of course, Father. I won't breathe a word."

"Good. Now tell me this: Can the Church be deceived?"

"The Church? Oh, no, Father."

"What about the Pope, the Vicar of Jesus Christ, when he speaks as Head of the Church?"

"No, he can't be deceived either."

Father Auvergne took a deep breath. The all-important question at last! "Maximin," he began cautiously, "suppose the Pope asked you to tell him your secret. You'd do it, wouldn't you?"

The boy shrugged, while a mischievous grin spread across his face. "I'm not in Rome where the Pope is. If I were . . . well, I'd see."

"What do you mean, you'd see?"

"Just what I said, Father. I'd see."

This answer was far too vague to suit Father Auvergne, but he decided not to press the point. "Well, son, suppose the Pope *ordered* you to tell him your secret," he continued casually. "What would you do?"

Maximin's eyes clouded. *"Ordered* me, Father?"

"That's right. You'd obey him, wouldn't you, as Head of the Church?"

There was a moment's silence. Then the boy nodded slowly. "I . . . I suppose so."

"You mean you'd tell him everything?"

"Yes."

"But what if you couldn't see him personally and he still wanted to know the secret?"

"Why, I'd put it in a sealed letter and send it to him, of course."

Relieved beyond words by the promptness of the reply, Father Auvergne offered a prayer of thanksgiving.

To think that the first part of his difficult mission had been accomplished so easily! Why, it was almost like a miracle! However, something told him he ought not to question Maximin any further just now. It was enough that he had sounded out the boy and found him willing to write down his secret for the Holy Father if ordered to do so.

"If only Melanie cooperates as well!" he thought hopefully.

However, when he arrived at the Motherhouse of the Sisters of Providence in Corenc, Father Auvergne soon realized that there was serious trouble ahead. Melanie, now nineteen years old, was as timid and fearful as when she had lived in the world. She would not dream of sharing her secret with anyone, even Pope Pius the Ninth.

"But the Pope, as Head of the Church, has the right to ask you to do just that, child," he pointed out kindly. "Why be so afraid?"

Melanie shook her head stubbornly. "No, the Blessed Virgin said I mustn't speak about it to anyone, Father."

"But how are we to know it was really the Blessed Virgin who appeared to you until the Church says so?"

The girl shifted awkwardly. "Oh, it was, Father! No one else could be so beautiful . . . or disappear so quickly into thin air."

"Ah, the Devil can do wonderful things, too, Melanie. You know that."

For a moment the girl was silent. Then tears flooded her eyes and she began to cry as though her heart would break. "All right, let the Church say it was the Devil!" she sobbed. "I don't care...."

Father Auvergne stretched out a reassuring hand. "But the Church can't make a decision until all the facts are known. Now, won't you help us? Won't you tell the Holy Father your secret?"

"I can't! I can't!"

"It's your duty, child. It's what the Blessed Virgin would like."

"B-but she said...."

"Don't forget that the Holy Father takes the place of her Son upon earth. She wants you to obey Pope Pius as though he were Jesus Christ Himself."

Melanie made a feeble attempt to wipe her tearful eyes. "B-but I'm so afraid...."

"There's no need to be. Just remember that when we obey the Holy Father, we're pleasing the Blessed Virgin. That's simple enough, isn't it?"

"Y-yes...."

"Then you'll tell Pope Pius your secret?"

Once again Melanie hesitated, twisting her hands nervously. "If ... if I have to," she said finally, in a choked voice. "But not anyone else, Father. Not anyone else in the whole world!"

Father Auvergne nodded encouragingly. "Of course not, child. You'll write Pope Pius a nice letter and explain everything. Then, in a little while...."

"IT'D BE A BIG SIN, FATHER!"

But without warning Melanie was in tears again. No, she would not put her secret in writing. Someone would be sure to read it before it reached the Holy Father. She would not confide in anyone but Pope Pius himself.

"It wouldn't be right!" she sobbed. "It'd be a big sin!"

Perplexed and not a little confused, Father Auvergne realized there was no use in prolonging the discussion. He would talk again with Melanie when she was less nervous and upset. However, the second interview was no more successful than the first, and presently Father Auvergne was on his way back to Grenoble in a depressed frame of mind.

"What's to be done now?" he asked himself. "The Bishop is going to be so disappointed!"

However, Bishop de Bruillard was far from being disappointed. In fact, he was quite satisfied with the way things had turned out. After all, hadn't both children agreed to tell their secrets to the Pope— Maximin in writing and Melanie in person? This was far more than many of his advisers had dared to hope.

"But Melanie can't go to Rome to speak to Pope Pius when she's in training to be a religious!" objected Father Auvergne. "Oh, if I could have just won her confidence, Your Lordship! Then our troubles would be about over. But this way—"

The Bishop smiled encouragingly. "Don't worry, Father. You've done splendid work in getting our two young friends to realize what's required of them. Perhaps in a few days. . . ."

"Yes, Your Lordship? You have something else in mind?"

"Well, I've been thinking of sending Father Rousselot to see Melanie, too. With God's help, he may be able to carry on very nicely where you left off."

CHAPTER TWENTY

FIVE DAYS later Father Rousselot left Grenoble for Corenc. And to the relief and joy of everyone, his trip was a success. After hours of painstaking effort, he had finally brought Melanie around to his way of thinking. True, she was still timid and full of doubts, but she had agreed to put her secret in writing, place it in a sealed envelope and give it to Father Rousselot to take to Pope Pius in Rome.

"Splendid, Father!" exclaimed Bishop de Bruillard. "I knew you'd be able to explain things to our little friend."

But Father Rousselot shook his head doubtfully. "I didn't do much, Your Lordship. It was really prayer that worked this miracle. And we're probably going to need a lot more before we're through."

The Bishop agreed. Yes, the Devil was far from pleased that devotion to Our Lady of La Salette might soon receive official recognition from Rome, and permission be given for the erection of a basilica on the site of the apparition. Undoubtedly there would be all kinds of trouble during the next few weeks.

"Well, we'll just keep on with our prayers," he said. "That's always the wisest thing to do."

Soon, because of Father Rousselot's successful trip to Corenc, there was considerable activity at the Bishop's house. If the children's secrets were to be taken to Rome, a report of the intensive study which had been made of the apparition during the past four and one-half years must go along, too. After all, if official approval was to be given, it was most necessary that the Holy Father possess a complete account of the many interviews in which the young shepherds had figured, especially those conducted by the Bishop's committee in November, 1847, and the more recent one in October, 1850, when Maximin had been called upon to explain his actions at Ars.

"All this work is going to take several weeks at least," the Bishop told Father Rousselot. "I don't think you'll be able to leave for Rome until May, Father. And when you do go. . . ."

"Yes, Your Lordship?"

"I think Father Gerin ought to go with you. As rector of the Cathedral here, what he has to say about the apparition will carry considerable weight."

However, it was not until the end of June that all
the documents were in readiness and arrangements
made for the children to write their secrets. By now
it had been agreed upon that Maximin should be the
first to testify. On July 2 he would be brought from
the Minor Seminary to a secluded room on the second
floor of the Bishop's house, where the learned Canon
de Taxis and Inspector Dausse (a well-known civil
engineer and a truly pious man), would witness his
efforts. Later in the day the Inspector would go to
Corenc to superintend the writing of Melanie's letter.

Naturally Canon de Taxis and his lay companion were much impressed with the important task
entrusted to them. But when July 2 finally arrived,
Maximin was far from sharing in their concern. Casually he entered the assigned room, gazed about a
moment, seated himself at a desk well removed from
his two witnesses, investigated the paper, envelopes,
pen and ink provided for him, then grinned impishly.
True, a moment later he did seem to reflect a little,
his face buried in his hands. But all too soon he had
seized a sheet of paper, plunged his pen into the ink,
shaken it out on the floor and begun a hasty scrawl.

Canon de Taxis was not a little disturbed by such
carelessness. "Maximin," he said sternly, "this is
the Bishop's house. What do you mean by being so
untidy?"

The boy looked at the inkspot on the floor, shrugged
and smiled. "Oh, that's nothing," he observed. "It'll
soon dry up."

For a moment all was silence in the room, save for the scratching of pen on paper. Then suddenly Maximin sprang up from his desk and approached Inspector Dausse. "How's this for a beginning?" he asked cheerfully.

Glancing at the few scrawled lines, the Inspector immediately noted that they did not concern the secret, only the familiar fact that on September 19, 1846, Maximin Giraud had seen a beautiful lady near La Salette.

"Very good," he said. "But take your time, son. There's no need to hurry."

However, it was soon evident that Maximin planned to finish his task as quickly as possible. Words were darting from his scratching pen, amid numerous blots, as though the boy were copying them from an open book. Then suddenly there was an odd silence.

The two witnesses exchanged anxious glances. Maximin's pen was poised in mid-air! "Yes, what is it?" they asked with one voice. "What's the trouble?"

The boy grinned. "I don't know how to spell 'pontiff.'"

The men experienced a sense of relief. So that was all! The restless lad before them had not had an unexpected scruple about writing his secret. . . .

"P-o-n-t-i-f-f," said the Canon in a clear voice. "Anything else, son?"

Maximin shook his head. Then he dipped his pen vigorously into the ink and resumed his narrative. But in just a few minutes he had paused again, folded his paper in two, thrown it high in the air, and with a hop, skip and jump had crossed the room to the open window.

"There, I'm through!" he exclaimed gaily. "I'm like everyone else now. If people want to know about the secret, they can bother the Pope, not me."

The Canon and his lay companion stared in dismay. Surely the famous secret hadn't been written in so short a time! And surely that smudged, untidy paper lying on the floor wasn't intended for the Holy Father!

"Maximin, hadn't you better make a good copy of your letter?" suggested the Inspector kindly. "After all, we do want things nice for the Pope."

The boy yawned, stretched and leaned far out the window to see what was going on down in the street. "No, I'm tired now," he declared. "What I've written is good enough."

Such a lack of manners shocked Canon de Taxis. "Maximin, do what you're told!" he ordered. "From what I can see of your letter, it's a disgrace. The Holy Father will never believe you've been studying for the priesthood if you send him that."

Very reluctantly Maximin turned from the window and came back to his desk. "Well, it's not a bit fair," he grumbled. "I never promised to write the Pope twice."

But the Canon was firm. A much neater copy of the letter must be made. And at once.

CHAPTER TWENTY-ONE

A N HOUR or so later, Maximin's second copy was placed in an envelope (whereon the witnesses had signed a statement that it was actually the boy's own work), closed with the official seal of the diocese and given to Bishop de Bruillard for safekeeping. Then Inspector Dausse set out to see Melanie at Corenc. God willing, her secret would soon be on paper, too. But when he arrived at the Motherhouse of the Sisters of Providence, he was met with bad news. Melanie was very upset. She had been crying for hours, and not even the chaplain could do anything with her.

"She's changed her mind about writing to Pope Pius," said the Mother Superior. "And when we tell her that she *must* see you sometime, Inspector—"

The latter nodded understandingly. "Don't worry, Mother. The Devil's just plaguing the poor child with a lot of foolish scruples. I'll talk to her at once."

"But—"

"There, there, everything's going to be all right. The sooner we settle those scruples, the better."

So presently nineteen-year-old Melanie was ushered into the convent parlor where the Inspector awaited her. But nothing could bring the girl to change her mind. It would be a big sin to disobey the Blessed Virgin and tell the secret, she declared tearfully. It would be enough to send a person to hell.

"Why, I thought all that was settled long ago, child," said the Inspector kindly. "Didn't Father Rousselot explain everything when he was here in March? And didn't you give him your word then that you'd write to the Holy Father?"

"Y-yes, sir," muttered Melanie, her lips quivering. "But I've thought a lot about things since, and now . . . well, I'm not going to do it!"

In vain the Inspector argued and pleaded. Melanie, her head bowed, her hands clasped tightly together, would not give in.

"No, no!" she sobbed. "It wouldn't be right!"

Finally the Inspector decided to let the girl rest. She was so tired and overwrought! Perhaps towards evening she would feel better and he would be able to get her to listen to reason.

"In the meantime, we'd better start praying again," he told the Mother Superior. "Otherwise the Devil is certainly going to win this battle."

THE SECOND COPY WAS PLACED IN AN ENVELOPE.

However, succeeding periods of questioning that night brought no results. Then suddenly the Inspector hit upon a plan. "All right," he told Melanie cheerfully. "I won't bother you any more, child. You may go now."

An expression of joyful relief crossed the girl's tear-stained face. "Y-you mean it, sir?" she whispered. "I don't have to tell my secret after all?"

The Inspector nodded. "Of course not, my dear. Since we can't give Pope Pius all the facts he needs, it must be the Will of God that Our Lady isn't to be officially honored on the holy mountain."

"B-but—"

"It's all right, Melanie. Thousands of people are going to be very pleased about this. You see, they've never approved of our plan to build a grand church in Our Lady's honor at La Salette. And when they hear that Bishop de Bruillard is going to let the whole matter drop. . . ."

"Oh, but he mustn't do that!"

"Why not?"

"Because . . . because Our Lady deserves a nice church."

"Nonsense! We can pray to her at home. Or in the little wooden chapel on the mountain."

"But the chapel's far too small for the pilgrims, sir! Only a few can get in it at a time."

"Well, what of that? There won't be many pilgrims coming from now on, child. After all, when people hear that the Holy Father isn't in favor of Bishop de Bruillard's publishing the pastoral letter he had in mind—a letter that was to be read in the six hundred churches and chapels of the diocese, Melanie, urging everyone to have a great devotion to Our Lady of La Salette—"

"But why wouldn't he want the Bishop to publish the letter?"

The Inspector shrugged. "How can Pope Pius be interested in what's going on at La Salette when he doesn't have the complete facts? Oh, no. He'll never approve of something he doesn't know all about. And naturally the Bishop will respect his wishes and not write the pastoral letter." Then, after a moment: "But don't worry, child. The new church would have cost a great deal of money. Now even our enemies will agree that we're being sensible in not having it built. And they'll be even more pleased when people stop believing in the apparition and there aren't any more pilgrimages to La Salette."

Melanie's eyes clouded with dismay. How dreadful if Our Lady wasn't to be honored on the holy mountain! If her message about keeping Sundays properly and not using bad language was to be scoffed at and forgotten! Terrible things would surely happen, just as she had forewarned nearly five years ago.

"If my people will not submit, I shall be forced to let go the hand of my Son. It is so strong, so heavy, that I can no longer withhold it. . . ."

Seeing that Melanie had lapsed into a prolonged silence and that she was more disturbed than ever about something, the Inspector rose to his feet. "Child, it's time you were in bed," he said kindly. "You've had a long, hard day. Run along now. And don't worry about anything. What's happened is just the Will of God."

Melanie hesitated, then shook her head. "No, I don't want to go to bed."

"But you must. It's very late, and you have to be up in time for Mass in the morning."

The girl wiped away her tears. "That's all right. I'll be up." Then, after a moment, and in a voice that was little more than a choked whisper: "Maybe . . . maybe after all I could write to Pope Pius, sir, and tell him my secret."

The Inspector's eyes shot open with astonishment. "What?"

"Yes, I mean it. You see, I just couldn't bear it if nothing more was done about La Salette. And this way—"

The Inspector was silent, scarcely daring to believe his ears. Then presently he managed a carefree smile. "Why, that would be fine," he said cheerfully. "When would you like to write to him, my dear? Tomorrow after Mass?"

Melanie nodded, her face the picture of woe. "Yes, sir. I guess so. . . ."

CHAPTER TWENTY-TWO

TO THE relief and joy of everyone at Corenc, Melanie wrote her long-delayed letter to Pope Pius the Ninth the next morning in the office of the convent chaplain. Surprisingly enough, she was quite calm and self-possessed. Words came to her easily, and she did not even trouble to read over her efforts.

"There, I've written the whole of my secret," she told Inspector Dausse when she had placed her letter in a sealed envelope. "You'll give it to Father Rousselot?"

The Inspector made no attempt to hide his satisfaction. "Of course, my dear. My, how pleased he's going to be that you've decided to help us! And the Holy Father, too." Then, a trifle hesitantly: "But suppose

Pope Pius decides to tell others what you've told him. Is that going to bother you?"

The girl shook her head, "Oh, no, sir. That will be his own affair."

"You won't mind at all?"

"Why should I? My part in things is finished now."

The convent chaplain (who had been present during the writing of the letter) was dumbfounded. What a change had come over Melanie! Why, this time yesterday she had been almost hysterical at the thought of putting her secret on paper! Now—

"Our prayers have certainly been answered," he told Inspector Dausse when they were alone. "Those wretched scruples that were plaguing the poor child have entirely disappeared."

"Yes, Father," replied the Inspector. "I guess the Devil's given up for the Time being."

"For the time being? Then you expect more trouble?"

"Why not? The Evil One's surely going to try again to keep Our Lady from being honored on the holy mountain."

"You don't mean Pope Pius will make light of the children's secrets!"

"Oh, no. But there'll be troubles of various sorts before there's a total acceptance of the apparition of Our Lady at La Salette. Mark my words."

Convinced though he was of this fact, the Inspector was quite unprepared for the urgent message which presently arrived at the Bishop's house in Grenoble from the Motherhouse of the Sisters of Providence in

Corenc. Melanie's letter, it seemed, obtained at such great cost, must not go to Rome after all. For some reason or other, she was not entirely satisfied with it.

"The child's either forgotten something important or she didn't make things quite clear in one place," announced the Bishop. "Now it seems she wants to write a second letter."

The Inspector's heart sank. What a disappointment for Fathers Rousselot and Gerin, whose trip to Rome must now be postponed indefinitely! As for himself—

"No," said the Bishop, reading his thoughts, "you don't have to go to Corenc again. Melanie will come here this time. She can write her letter at some convent in the city."

Soon there was great excitement when it became known that Melanie had arrived in Grenoble. What exactly was the trouble? Surely the girl hadn't lied about something in the first letter, or been bothered with scruples again! But it was not until July 6 that anyone could be sure. On that day, in the local house of the Sisters of Providence in Grenoble, in the presence of Mother Saint Louis, the superior, and Father Auvergne, the Bishop's secretary, Melanie wrote to Pope Pius the Ninth for the second time.

When all was over, both witnesses were overwhelmed with questions. Just what had been the trouble? Had Melanie given any explanation as to why she had wanted to write a second letter? Had there been any clues as to her famous secret? Had she seemed unduly upset or depressed? Had she had any difficulty in expressing her thoughts?

"No, it was all very simple," said Father Auvergne, speaking for Mother Saint Louis as well as for himself. "Apparently the first time Melanie wrote to Pope Pius, she mentioned two events which Our Lady told her are to take place, but she put down only one date."

"She should have given two separate dates?"

"Yes."

"Anything else?"

"Well, she did ask the meaning of the world 'infallibly.' A little later on she wanted to know how to spell 'soiled' and 'Antichrist.'"

"And that's all?"

"Yes."

"Was it a big effort for the girl to write this second letter?"

"Oh, no. Melanie seemed very composed. She wrote quite rapidly, as though she knew just what she wanted to say."

"The letter was long?"

"Yes, several pages."

However, when the questions began to turn upon the secret, both witnesses had to admit to complete ignorance. Melanie had told them nothing. She had not even seen fit to mention the two dates which had caused all the confusion. They were part of the secret, she said, and only the Pope was to know them.

"Well, we'll just have to wait until Fathers Rousselot and Gerin come back from Rome," people told one another. "Perhaps the Holy Father will show them what's in the children's letters and give permission to let us know, too."

The two priests cherished the same hope, and lost no time in setting out on their trip—arriving in the Eternal City on July 11. However, it was not until July 18 that an interview could be arranged for them with Pope Pius. Then, eager and hopeful, they presented themselves at the Vatican.

"So, Fathers, at last you've come about La Salette," said Pope Pius when he had greeted them warmly and read the letter of introduction brought from Bishop de Bruillard. "Here in Rome we've heard a great deal about the apparition, of course. But as for the so-called secrets. . . ."

Father Rousselot's pulse quickened. "Melanie and Maximin have each written to you, Your Holiness. I think their letters will tell you everything."

The Pope smiled. "Well, let me see these letters."

Scarcely daring to breathe, Father Rousselot presented the two sealed envelopes, then stepped back a respectful distance and glanced at Father Gerin. The great moment at last! What would it finally bring forth?

CHAPTER TWENTY-THREE

IT WAS Maximin's letter which Pope Pius read first. And as the Bishop's two envoys stood watching in tense silence, eager for some clue as to its contents, a smile crossed his face.

"Here is certainly all the simplicity of a child," he murmured.

However, when he had returned the letter to its envelope and had begun to read what Melanie had written, his lips tightened and his expression changed to grim concern. Seemingly this second letter was far more impressive than the first, and the two priests exchanged anxious glances. Could it be that Melanie's secret dealt with some great trial in store for the Church? A persecution, perhaps? Or dreadful sufferings even for those outside the Church who believed in God and tried to serve Him?

However, when he had finished reading Melanie's letter, Pope Pius did not see fit to make any enlightening comment. In fact, the few words he did speak had an air of mystery about them, too.

"Calamities threaten France, but she is not the only guilty country," he observed. "Germany, Italy and all Europe are guilty, and deserve punishment. I have less to fear from open impiety than from indifference and human respect . . . It is not without reason that the Church is called militant." Then, pointing to himself with his right hand: "And here you see her leader."

The two priests nodded silently, eager to hear more. But there was no more. His Holiness would read both letters again, he said, pray and think about them, then consult with his advisers. In the meantime, Fathers Rousselot and Gerin would make themselves at home, and enjoy their visit to the Eternal City?

Realizing that the interview was over, the Bishop's envoys respectfully took their departure. Doubtless Pope Pius would make known his opinion in the not too distant future. For the time being, they must be content with the fact that they had done their duty. It was also consoling to know that a book which Father Rousselot had written about La Salette had been read and approved by one of the most learned men in Rome—Bishop Frattini, the Promoter of the Faith.

"Actually things are going very well for us," declared Father Gerin presently. "All we have to do now is to pray and be patient, and they'll probably go still better."

True enough. As the days passed, it became quite evident that many important people in Rome had a great interest in La Salette. Among these were several Cardinals who saw no reason why Bishop de Bruillard should not issue his pastoral letter, authorizing public devotion to Our Lady of La Salette, then begin plans for the building of a church in her honor on the holy mountain. One prelate in particular, Cardinal Lambruschini, Prefect of the Sacred Congregation of Rites, was more than enthusiastic. The Holy Father had permitted him to read the children's letters, and ever since then his belief in the apparition had taken on added fervor.

"Fathers, everything's going to turn out all right," he said. "One of these days there'll be good news to take back to Grenoble. Just wait and see."

The Cardinal was right. Word finally came from the Vatican that Bishop de Bruillard might proceed as he saw fit concerning the publishing of his letter and the building of a fine, new church at La Salette. There was no doubt but that five years ago Our Lady had appeared to Melanie Mathieu and Maximin Giraud. And the message which she had given—that Sunday must be kept holy and that people must not use bad language or take' the Name of God in vain—ought to be heard and understood by all, and commemorated in a fitting manner.

Eighty-six-year-old Bishop de Bruillard was jubilant. What splendid news! Now that Rome had spoken, it would certainly be in order for him to pay his first visit to the holy mountain. Perhaps he would go on September 19, the fifth anniversary of the apparition. On the other hand, because of his poor health and the likelihood of autumn storms, it might be wiser to postpone the trip to the following May, when the weather would be comparatively mild and the plans for laying of the first stone for the new church completed.

"That would be best, Your Lordship," agreed his advisers presently. "After all, it's a long and tiring trip to La Salette. You don't want to take any unnecessary chances."

But even as he pondered the matter, another problem confronted the Bishop. The secrets! Everyone was anxious to know what the children had written in their letters to Pope Pius the Ninth. Gossip had it that Our Lady had prophesied dreadful things to Melanie, because of the sins of the world, but that she had spoken more cheerfully to Maximin. To him she had described the mercy of God toward those who kept the Commandments and did penance. It was this, people said, which accounted for the girl's tendency to sadness and the boy's light-heartedness and easy-going ways. Now if only some official statement could be forthcoming from the Bishop's house, so as to settle matters once and for all—

"But what *can* be said, definitely, about the secrets?" the Bishop asked himself from time to time. "Absolutely nothing, of course. Pope Pius never saw fit to confide in Father Rousselot or Father Gerin. And the children still won't say a word."

It was true. Neither Melanie nor Maximin would discuss what Our Lady had told them, not even with the Cardinal Archbishop of Lyons, who had made a special trip to see them in July. Nevertheless, after his return from Rome, Father Gerin had the rare experience of obtaining one slight clue when he went to visit Melanie at Corenc.

"Child, I don't know what you wrote to the Holy Father," he told her, "but he seemed much affected by it."

Melanie smiled, and so radiantly, that the priest could not take his eyes from her face. But as she remained silent, he continued casually: "Whatever it was, I don't think it was very flattering."

"Flattering!" exclaimed Melanie, still smiling.

"Yes. Do you know what that word means?"

The girl nodded. "Oh, yes, Father. It means to give pleasure. But what I wrote ought to give pleasure to the Pope. A Pope ought to love to suffer."

Father Gerin looked up sharply. "What's that, child? What did you say?"

But Melanie shook her head and refused to comment further. She would not even discuss a statement which she had made several times in the past: namely, that as Our Lady had disappeared into the

THE BISHOP WAS JUBILANT.

sky on September 19, 1846, her sorrowful gaze had seemed to be turned toward the east—and Rome.

"Hmm, very interesting," observed the Bishop, when he had heard the story. "But we certainly can't make an official statement that the Pope ought to love to suffer."

"No," admitted Father Gerin. "I don't suppose we can."

CHAPTER TWENTY-FOUR

O N OCTOBER 10, 1851, all those interested in the progress of devotion to Our Lady of La Salette were delighted to hear that Melanie had received the habit of a Sister of Providence. Henceforth she would be known as Sister Mary of the Cross. Of course just now she was only a novice, but there was good reason to believe that in three years' time—when she had made her vows—she would be sent to the foreign missions. Maximin had also expressed a desire to work in pagan lands. However, he was no longer studying at the Minor Seminary of Grenoble. So many visitors had been coming to see him there that his work had suffered. Now it had been decided to enroll him at Saint Andrew's, a small country school for ecclesiastical students.

"God willing, the lad will do far better with his studies from now on," was the general opinion.

Bishop de Bruillard shared the same hope as he applied himself to what had been in his thoughts for so long: the writing of the pastoral letter approving public devotion to Our Lady of La Salette. This was published on November 16. Then early the following May he issued a second letter, announcing the purchase of a tract of land on the holy mountain which included the exact spot where Our Lady had appeared. A large church was to be built here, he said, and placed in charge of a group of priests who would be known as the Missionaries of La Salette. From May to November they would care for the needs of the pilgrims who came to honor Our Lady at her new shrine. Then, when the winter storms set in and there were no more pilgrimages, they would do priestly work among the scattered mountain communities.

The two letters brought joy to thousands of hearts, but not to the enemies of the Church.

"An elaborate shrine at La Salette?" they sneered. "Why, all this is only a scheme to make money! Just wait and see."

"That's right. Those new missionaries are out to make a fancy profit from the pilgrims."

"Naturally the Bishop has the same idea."

"Of course. That old man's no fool. He knows a good business deal when he sees one."

"Why not, after having lived eighty-six years?"

But despite all the slander and malicious gossip, plans went steadily forward for the erection of the new shrine. Offerings, large and small, began to arrive from all parts of France, and even from foreign countries. Finally May 25, 1852, was chosen as the day for the blessing of the land and the laying of the first stone. However, it was regretfully announced that Bishop Peter Chatrousse of Valence would preside at the ceremony instead of the Bishop of Grenoble. The latter was now in such poor health that even though the fine spring days were at hand, the trip to La Salette would probably prove too much for him.

Poor Bishop de Bruillard! He was very disappointed at the thought of having to miss the great celebration. How hard he had worked to make everything possible! How eagerly he had looked forward to honoring Our Lady at her new shrine!

"I've never even seen the holy mountain," he told himself sadly, recalling that somehow it had never seemed quite proper to go there until Pope Pius had decided that the Blessed Virgin had actually appeared to the children. And now, when everything was finally settled—

"Never mind, Your Lordship, you'll be able to visit La Salette some other time," consoled his advisers. "Later in the summer, quietly and at your leisure...."

The Bishop smiled ruefully. "No, Fathers, I don't think I'll ever see the summer. Somehow I feel my days on earth are just about over."

The advisers lapsed into uneasy silence, for the same thought had occurred to them. Not only was the Bishop eighty-six years of age, and badly crippled with rheumatism. His heart was none too strong either, and frequently even a short walk in the garden produced an alarming spell of dizziness and shortness of breath.

"His Lordship's right," they decided privately. "He'll probably never see La Salette, except from heaven."

Then, shortly before the scheduled celebration, Bishop de Bruillard startled everyone by saying that he was going to the holy mountain after all. The Bishop of Valence could attend to the day's more arduous ceremonies—such as the singing of the Solemn High Mass and the giving of Benediction—but he himself must have some small share in things, too. He would offer a low Mass in the little wooden chapel, then bless the first stone of the new church.

Everyone was aghast. "But it's thirty-seven miles from Grenoble to La Salette, Your Lordship! And over the worst possible roads!"

"Then another mile up the mountain to the place of the apparition, with no road at all!"

"If it rains, the place'll be nothing but a sea of mud!"

"Oh, you just can't think of making such a hard trip!"

"And certainly not while fasting!"

The Bishop smiled. "Don't worry. I considered all these things when I made my plans. Now everything's settled. I'm going to leave here by stagecoach on May 24, then stop over at Corps for a good night's rest. Very early the next morning I'll be off for La Salette."

The advisers looked at one another in dismay. Had the Bishop taken leave of his senses? The five-mile trip from Corps to La Salette was no easy journey, even for a person in good health. As for the mile-long climb up the mountainside to the site of the apparition—

"It's all right," said the Bishop, reading their thoughts. "I know the stagecoach can't go up the mountain, so I'm going up on horseback."

All the anxious protests of his advisers were in vain; the Bishop set out on his pilgrimage on May 24. And what a sight greeted his eyes when he arrived at the little wooden chapel on the holy mountain about eight o'clock the next morning! Some fifteen thousand men and women were on hand, many of whom had spent the entire night in the open, asking the blessing of God's Mother on themselves and their families. Now, as they realized that their beloved shepherd was with them after all, the air echoed to a thunderous welcome.

"Long live His Lordship!"

"Long live Bishop de Bruillard!"

"God bless our Bishop!"

"May the Holy Mother protect him!"

Worn though he was, and weak from hunger, the Bishop experienced such a thrill of joy that tears streamed down his cheeks. How good to be in this holy place! How well worth all the pain and fatigue of his journey! Then presently, as he began the Holy Sacrifice, it almost seemed as though he were in heaven itself. Such faith on the part of the pilgrims! Such love of God! Such peace! Surely this obscure mountainside where Our Lady had appeared was the most blessed spot in his whole diocese? As for May 25, 1852—ah, without doubt it was one of the happiest days in his whole life. . . .

"Dearest Lord, thank You for letting me be here!" he prayed over and over again. "Thank You so much!"

In just a little while those in charge of the day's proceedings observed with dismay that heavy clouds were gathering over the mountain, with jagged flashes of lightning cutting through the sky from time to time, followed by ominous peals of thunder. A bad storm was surely in the making which threatened to ruin the entire celebration.

"We'd better start praying to Our Lady to send some good weather," was the general decision.

But by ten o'clock a light drizzle had already begun to fall. An umbrella was hastily procured for the use of Bishop Chatrousse as he emerged from the little wooden chapel to bless the site of the new church. Another sheltered Bishop de Bruillard as he blessed and laid the first stone. Then, although the drizzle presently turned into a real shower, the great crowd remained in silent attention during the High Mass which followed, the sermon by Father Sibillat (one of the three newly-appointed Missionaries of

La Salette), and Solemn Benediction of the Blessed Sacrament.

However, as noon approached and the long ceremonies finally came to an end, the people grew more anxious. Apparently it had been the Blessed Virgin's wish that penance be added to prayer on this historic occasion, and so the earnest request for good weather had gone unanswered. But now—

"What about Bishop de Bruillard?" was the question on everyone's lips. "The poor old man must be tired out. And chilled to the bone by the dampness."

"That's right. And suffering more than ever from his rheumatism."

"How's he going to get back to Corps? He'll never be able to ride a horse down the pilgrim path now."

It was true. Owing to the morning's storm and the trampling of thousands of feet, the entire mountainside had become a sea of slippery mud. No horse could keep its footing on the treacherous trails that led to Corps and La Salette. And though for the moment the rain had ceased, it was by no means over.

"Well, we'll just have to get some men to carry him down in a chair," was the final decision.

"*Carry him!* But it's a whole mile to La Salette! And if the men should ever stumble and fall—"

"No matter. We'll have to take that chance. It's the only thing we can do."

CHAPTER TWENTY-FIVE

SOON, SEATED in an arm chair under a canvas canopy, the whole topped by hastily-cut boughs and branches, the aged Bishop of Grenoble was being carried down the mountain by four stalwart young men. Before him and behind streamed thousands of pilgrims, praying and singing, their sodden parish banners held high in the air, while in the distance echoed the melodious chimes from the little church of La Salette.

Even while they prayed and sang, the pilgrims watched their Bishop with anxious care. Had the day's excitement been too much for him? Would he be able to rally from the strain? Certainly just now he was very pale and worn, scarcely able to lift his hand in blessing over the crowds that pressed about him. And though his bearers were proceeding with extreme vigilance, at times they could not help jolting him severely.

"And it's six miles to Corps!" one person reminded another anxiously.

"Yes, then the long ride by stagecoach to Grenoble!"

"Oh, the poor Bishop! It'll be a wonder if he lives through the day!"

But Bishop de Bruillard was so happy over the morning's great events that he scarcely noticed the hardship of the journey. Indeed, when he finally arrived home, he found himself possessed of a remarkable new energy.

"Our Lady's responsible," he told his astonished advisers. "Why, I haven't felt this well in months!"

To everyone's delight, the Bishop was able to attend to his numerous duties throughout the summer and fall of 1852 without ill effect—offering Mass each day, receiving visitors, writing letters, holding conferences, and doing everything possible to foster devotion at Our Lady's new shrine. But shortly after his eighty-seventh birthday (on December 15), his health failed again, and presently he had retired to a convent of the Religious of the Sacred Heart at nearby Montfleury. God willing, the able Vicar General of Aix, Monsignor Ginoulhiac, would take his place as Bishop of Grenoble.

Of course no one could begrudge the aged prelate his well-earned rest. For most of his long life he had been laboring for the spiritual welfare of others—thirty-seven years as a priest, twenty-six years as a Bishop—and although he would be sorely missed in Grenoble, it was only fitting that he spend his last days in carefree retirement. And how consoling that he was going to live at Montfleury! The Religious of the Sacred Heart would surely give him every attention, for had he not once been the spiritual director of their beloved foundress, Mother Madeleine Sophie Barat?

Unfortunately the enemies of the Church took advantage of Bishop de Bruillard's resignation to begin a new and most vicious attack against La Salette. Before May 7, 1853, when Bishop-elect Ginoulhiac arrived in Grenoble to assume his episcopal duties, they had announced that Melanie and Maxi min, far from enjoying a heavenly vision on September 19, 1846, had merely seen and talked with Constance Louise Lamerlière, a pious and wealthy lady from Saint Marcellin, who had been visiting in the neighborhood at the time. This woman's gentle speech, gracious manners and beautiful clothes had so impressed the ignorant little shepherds that they had innocently decided she must be the Mother of God. As for the so-called miraculous spring? It was slowly drying up. The hundreds of people who claimed to have been cured of this or that ailment after praying on the holy mountain? Poor souls, they only imagined they were feeling better.

"What nonsense!" Father Rousselot told Father Gerin when the news broke. "Why, Constance Louise Lamerlière was seventy-five miles away from

IT WAS SIX MILES TO CORPS. . . .

La Salette the day Our Lady appeared! She's been telling that to everyone she meets."

"Yes, and who'd ever mistake her for the Blessed Virgin? Certainly such a short, plump little woman would never be able to walk on top of the grass blades without bending them!"

"Why, it'd be a chore for her to climb even half-way up the mountain!"

"That's right. Oh, this is the most ridiculous story yet!"

"It surely is. No one's ever going to believe it."

But many people did believe the malicious falsehood, especially after the story had appeared in pamphlet form and was being given wide publicity in the secular press. As a result, there was considerable scandal and much harm was done Our Lady's cause at La Salette. Then, even as Bishop Ginoulhiac pondered the best course of action to take, there came fresh cause for anxiety. Maximin, who had not done at all well with his studies at Saint Andrew's and so had recently returned to the Minor Seminary, was causing his teachers no little concern. What a light-headed, impossible youth! Although he was nearly eighteen, his knowledge of Latin and other important subjects was less than that of a boy of twelve.

"To make matters worse, he doesn't seem a bit worried about his poor standing," complained the professors. "He still says he'll make a good priest."

Bishop Ginoulhiac, new to his work and unwilling to take any drastic steps as yet, recommended patience. Maximin's background was very different from that of the other students at the Seminary. Both his parents were dead. What relatives he did have were only ignorant peasants. Surely it was unreasonable to expect too much from such a boy?

"Perhaps a trip to Rome might help him," he suggested one day. "Tell Maximin that if he settles down and does good work, we may be able to send him there next year."

Then presently there were other trials for Bishop Ginoulhiac. Melanie, now Sister Mary of the Cross, was not doing well at Corenc. Although she was extremely hard-working and devout, frequently she showed a type of independence that was not at all in keeping with the standards of a good religious. Her health was poor, and yet more often than not she refused to take the proper care of herself. Even worse. Although she loved children and had been given a class to teach, she was often in such a bad mood that she accomplished nothing with them. And she was far too strict. In fact, she was scarcely ever seen to smile or to show any other sign of happiness.

As he had in Maximin's case, the Bishop counseled patience. But in January, 1854, he was forced to agree with the superiors at Corenc. Sister Mary of the Cross needed special medical treatment and must go at once to Vienne. This was a town some fifty miles northwest of Grenoble where the Sisters of Charity had a comfortable rest house and excellent medical facilities. The climate was far milder than at

Corenc, too, and most sick people derived real benefit from a stay there.

However, in just three weeks there was distressing news from Vienne. Sister Mary of the Cross did not like her new quarters. She refused to cooperate with the doctors and nurses, was miserable and homesick, and wanted to come back to the Motherhouse. Above all, she longed for permission to visit Our Lady's new shrine at La Salette. If only she could make a pilgrimage there, she pleaded, her various ailments would vanish.

"Well, all right," agreed the Bishop reluctantly. "But all this is certainly most irregular. And if Sister Mary of the Cross expects to make her vows in October, she'd better start learning to set aside her own will. Without the virtues of humility and obedience, no one can be a good religious."

Having received the desired permission, Sister Mary of the Cross left Vienne, paid a visit to the holy mountain and returned to Corenc around the first of March. And, to everyone's joy and delight, in excellent health and spirits.

"Our Lady cured me at La Salette, just as I knew she would," she announced happily. "I'm quite all right now."

But soon the superiors decided that Melanie was not all right. True, she no longer suffered from the old aches and pains. She was prayerful, mortified and devoted to her teaching. But she was still inclined to frequent periods of moodiness, preferring to walk alone at recreation rather than to join in conversation with the other Sisters. In fact, there had been several instances when she had not spoken to anyone for days.

"It's as though she'd been stricken dumb," the Mother Superior told the Bishop. "And yet, if the chaplain blesses the poor child—"

The prelate looked up with concern. "Yes, Mother? What happens then?"

"Why, Sister Mary of the Cross begins to talk and act quite normally, as though nothing was the trouble. But in an hour or so she's just as apt to lapse into silence again. Or else she'll say and do the strangest things, as though she were not herself at all."

The Bishop hesitated. Could Melanie's unusual conduct mean that she was being cruelly tormented by the Devil? For reasons known only to God, such a trial had been experienced by certain chosen souls from the earliest ages of the Church. Already the convent chaplain, Father Gérente, had expressed a belief that this was true of Melanie. And other priests had said the same thing. Still—

"Mother, I think we'd better put our young friend to a test," he observed presently.

"A *test,* Your Lordship?"

"Yes. Melanie's quite attached to her teaching work, isn't she?"

"Oh, yes. Very attached. That's one reason she was so miserable at Vienne. She missed her pupils dreadfully."

"Well, attachment to one's work on the part of a religious can be a bad as well as a good thing. In Melanie's case, I've an idea it's bad. So I want you to take her away from her teaching. And from the Motherhouse, too. Give her the lowest place in the convent at Corps. Then see what happens."

The Mother Superior nodded calmly. The purpose of the Bishop's plan was only too evident. If Melanie satisfied the superiors at Corps, she would be allowed to make her vows in October and become a full-fledged member of the Sisters of Providence. If not—

"I'll see to things right away," she promised. "But perhaps, Your Lordship. . . ."

"Yes, Mother?"

"Well, I'm sure that Melanie needs prayers. Maybe you'd give her a remembrance these days? Especially at Mass?"

The Bishop's eyes softened. "Of course," he said kindly. "I'll pray very hard for Melanie, Mother. Be assured of that."

CHAPTER TWENTY-SIX

IT WAS around the first of May that Sister Mary of the Cross took up residence at Corps. And although she was given every consideration, so that her health remained good, the superiors were soon extremely worried on other scores. For instance, this young Sister was so unreliable! And how distressing that she sulked and fretted because she was no longer allowed to teach at the Motherhouse! Of course it was splendid that she was so prayerful and devout, spending long hours in the chapel each day. But what dark looks when she was asked to help out in the kitchen or the laundry, or to take a hand in some other menial task! To make matters worse, so-called friends were constantly stopping at the convent to sympathize with her in her imaginary woes, later spreading all manner of twisted stories. The poor child was not being fairly treated, they said. The superiors at Corenc were a cruel and heartless lot to have taken this little nun away from her beloved teaching. Bishop Ginoulhiac was no better. Certainly his predecessor would never have been so unkind.

As the weeks passed, things went from bad to worse. Then finally, in August, the regrettable decision had to be made. Melanie had no vocation to the Sisters of Providence. Apparently (as had been feared years ago by several in the community), a dangerous type of pride had crept into her soul and it would be unwise to allow her to make her vows in October. She had best leave the convent at once and return home.

"But what's going to become of the child?" Bishop Ginoulhiac asked his advisers anxiously. "Her people are only poor peasants, with scarcely enough to eat. And if Melanie should ever fall into the hands of the enemies of the Church. . . ."

No one had any suggestions. Then, shortly before September 19, Bishop Newsham from England came forward with an idea. He and some friends were in the neighborhood hoping to celebrate the eighth anniversary of Our Lady's apparition on the holy mountain. Hearing that Melanie was no longer in the convent, he had gone to visit her at home and had been deeply touched to find her so miserable and forlorn, misunderstood by friends and family alike. Half-jokingly he had asked if she wouldn't like to have a trip to England, and the girl had astounded him by her eagerness to go. Now, what did Bishop Ginoulhiac think? Was he in favor of the idea? After all, Maximin was about to have his trip to Rome. Doubtless Melanie would profit from a little vacation, too.

Bishop Ginhouliac scarcely knew what to say. A trip of five hundred miles or more, with all expenses paid? How kind of the English prelate to take such an interest in Melanie! But where would she stay in England? Who would look after her? How long would she be gone?

"Don't worry about details," said Bishop Newsham kindly. "I know the Carmelite Sisters in Darlington will be delighted to have Melanie as a guest—for one month, two months, six months—as long as she cares to stay."

The Bishop hesitated. "Darlington, Your Lordship? I've never heard of that town. Is it near London?"

"No, it's in northern England, near Durham. I know the place well, and the Sisters, too. They'll see that Melanie has every comfort, and that she isn't bothered with unwelcome publicity. Perhaps they can even teach her a little English."

A wave of relief filled Bishop Ginoulhiac's heart. All this was surely the answer to prayer! Away from France, in new and different surroundings, Melanie might be able to overcome many of her difficulties and discover what God wanted of her. And if she had some study to occupy her mind as well, such as learning to speak English, it would certainly keep her from unhealthy moping.

Everyone agreed that it would be the best thing for Melanie to leave France for a while. Recently there had been a great deal of unfortunate gossip about her dismissal from the convent. Then, too, there was that wretched story about Constance Louise Lamerlière's having pretended that it was she who had visited the children on September 19, 1846, not the Mother of God. In a few days the good woman planned to bring a lawsuit against those who had promoted this ridiculous falsehood. As a result, the secular press would be carrying all manner of questionable publicity about La Salette. Maximin would escape much of this by virtue of his absence in Rome. But Melanie, at home in Corps, the prey of one unscrupulous visitor after another. . . .

"Let the girl go to England," was the unanimous decision of the Bishop's advisers. "Under the circumstances, it's the very best thing she could do."

So, on September 20, the day following the eighth anniversary of Our Lady's apparition on the holy mountain, twenty-two-year-old Melanie set out for England with Bishop Newsham and his party. And in a week or so there was good news. The group had arrived safely, and Melanie was now happily established with the Carmelites in Darlington. The Sisters were very fond of their young French guest, and were doing all that they could to make her feel at home.

"Thank God!" exclaimed Bishop Ginoulhiac when he heard the news. "Our prayers for Melanie's happiness are certainly being answered."

Then, on December 8, there was fresh cause for rejoicing when Pope Pius the Ninth solemnly proclaimed the dogma of the Immaculate Conception of the Blessed Virgin Mary. Henceforth every loyal Catholic would accept without question the traditional belief that Our Lady's soul had never known the slightest stain of sin.

"How wonderful!" reflected the Bishop, as he watched the vast crowds pouring into the Cathedral of Grenoble to pay tribute to the Mother of God. "Why, the eighth of December is no longer just an ordinary winter's day but one of the greatest feast days in the Church!" Then, with a sudden and surprising confidence: "And surely the many prayers at La Salette have helped to bring it all about?"

CHAPTER TWENTY-SEVEN

A S THE weeks passed, the news concerning Melanie continued to be reassuring. She was happy in her new home, had learned quite a bit of English, and was much attached to the Carmelites and their way of life. Then presently came word that she had asked to be admitted to the community, so that she might spend the rest of her days in prayer and penance for sinners.

Bishop Ginoulhiac was extremely doubtful of this sudden vocation, and so were Father Rousselot and Father Gerin. Melanie seemed far from possessing the necessary strength and vitality for the difficult life of Carmel. In fact, her past record indicated that she was ill-suited to any kind of community life. Those spells of moodiness, for instance; the fits of sulking when she could not have her own way. More serious still, the occasions when she was mysteriously stricken dumb, or when she spoke and acted as though she were not herself.

However, when it became known that the superiors at Darlington were honestly convinced that Melanie would persevere as a Carmelite, Bishop Ginoulhiac refrained from all discouraging comment. And on February 25, 1855, when she was received as a postulant, he offered many fervent prayers that God would bless her in her new way of life.

"It *could* be that she has a vocation to Carmel," he admitted. "After all, she's a prayerful and devout girl in spite of her odd ways."

Then presently there was most astonishing news concerning Melanie. Shortly after her entrance into the cloister she had been stricken with blindness, but not long thereafter her sight had been restored through a miracle!

"What happened?" people asked one another excitedly. "How did she get better?"

No one could be sure of details, but soon the main facts were being pieced together.

"Melanie was blind for three weeks or so, and suffering dreadfully from headaches. The Prioress was very worried, and didn't know what to do. Then Sister Bridget, one of the holiest members of the community, died suddenly."

"Yes, yes! What happened then?"

"The nuns were offering the usual prayers for Sister Bridget, and preparing for the funeral, when someone suggested that it might be better to pray *to* the dead Sister rather than *for* her."

"But what's all this got to do with Melanie?"

"Well, it was decided that through her God might furnish a sign to prove that Sister Bridget had gone straight to heaven when she died."

"A sign?"

"That's right. Melanie was told to take the dead nun's hand, place it on her eyes, and ask God to show that Sister Bridget's long life in Carmel had been pleasing to Him and that she was now a saint in heaven."

"And that's what happened?"

"Yes. As soon as the girl had touched Sister Bridget's hand to her eyes and asked for a cure, she could see as well as ever."

"Well, that does sound like a miracle!"

"Sounds like one? It *is* one! Probably all sorts of English Protestants will be coming into the Church when they hear about it."

However, when pressed for an opinion on this point, neither Bishop Ginoulhiac nor his advisers would make any definite statement. True, there was a growing interest in Catholicism in England, especially since the conversion of three prominent Anglican clergymen: John Henry Newman and Frederick William Faber in 1845, then Henry Edward Manning in 1851. Moreover, devotion to Our Lady of La Salette was gaining considerable ground through the sermons of William Bernard Ullathorne, Bishop of Birmingham. He had visited the holy mountain only a few months

THERE HAD BEEN A MIRACLE IN CARMEL!

before and now was writing a book about his experiences. But as for Melanie's reported cure bringing anyone into the Church. . . .

"Miracles have their place, but prayer and suffering are the surest means to win graces for others," observed the Bishop prudently.

However, despite a seeming lack of interest in the so-called miracle, he continued to follow Melanie's progress in Carmel with keen attention, and was more than happy to learn that her health remained good and that the superiors were entirely satisfied with her. Only Maximin remained something of a problem. Now twenty-one years old, he was as backward as ever with his books, and the despair of all his professors because of his carefree ways.

"This young man will never make a priest," was their constant complaint. "He's far too fickle. And he can't seem to remember anything he reads."

Maximin merely shrugged off such comments. "I *am* going to be a priest," he insisted cheerfully. "What's more, I'm going to some foreign country and tell thousands of poor pagans about the day Our Lady appeared on the mountain and said that people mustn't work on Sundays or use bad language. They'll all listen to that story, and become converted, too."

As he had done from the beginning, Bishop Ginoulhiac counseled patience on the part of Maximin's teachers. But after a year or so he was forced to admit that the studies for the priesthood probably required a concentration of which the youth was incapable. Perhaps it would be better if he left the Seminary and went to work somewhere. In Paris there certainly ought to be an opening for him, in a hospital or some other charitable institution.

In the spring of 1858, as he was still considering the idea, there came exciting news from an obscure mountain village in southwestern France. Here, in Lourdes, Our Lady was said to be appearing again, this time to another poor little peasant by the name of Bernadette Soubirous. Her first visit had been on February 11, with several more occurring since. Among other things, she had told the fourteen-year-old girl that people must pray and do penance. Then, as though to prove that she really was the Blessed Virgin, that she really did come to help her children, a fountain had sprung up out of the dry ground whose waters possessed miraculous powers.

"In a way, it's the story of La Salette all over again," thought the Bishop, not without concern. For these new visits of Our Lady (and by July 16 there had been eighteen of them), could mean that not enough attention had been paid the message she had given Melanie and Maximin. Without doubt hundreds of thousands of people were still addicted to blasphemy, greed, drunkenness, impurity—even in so-called Christian countries. As for keeping Sundays holy and free from unnecessary servile work. . . .

"Things are not as bad as they were, but they're still not nearly good enough," the Bishop decided.

"And Catholics, who should know better, are just as much at fault as anyone."

What was to be done? Surely the answer lay in renewed prayer and penance on the part of both priests and people? In frequent meditation upon the words Our Lady had spoken at La Salette?

"If my people will not submit, I shall be forced to let go the hand of my Son. It is so strong, so heavy, that I can no longer withhold it. . . ."

The Bishop's advisers agreed heartily on this point, and all during the summer and fall of 1858 they promoted Our Lady's cause with an ever-increasing awareness of its importance. Thus on September 19, when it came time to celebrate the twelfth anniversary of her apparition at La Salette, there were ten thousand pilgrims on the holy mountain, some of whom had walked sixteen hours to be present! There were also ninety priests to offer the Holy Sacrifice in the partly finished new church.

Of course Bishop Ginoulhiac was pleased at all the honor being paid the Mother of God. At least huge numbers in the diocese of Grenoble were doing what they could to promote devotion to her, and to make reparation for sinners. But if only more could be done! If only other thousands could learn to love and trust her, to take her urgent messages to heart and act upon them!

"We'll have to pray for that," he told himself. "We'll have to pray very hard."

CHAPTER TWENTY-EIGHT

FERVENT PRAYER was offered by the Bishop that many more people would come to know and believe in the message of La Salette. And with gratifying results, for almost every day pilgrims from all parts of Europe were to be seen making their way up the holy mountain. Indeed, from time to time, there were devout souls praying in the new church who had come from such distant lands as Canada, Syria, the East Indies and Australia.

But it was not for this reason alone that in mid-October the Bishop's prayers developed into ones of thanksgiving rather than petition. Quite suddenly Father John Marie Vianney, the parish priest of Ars, reversed his decision with regard to La Salette! Once again the seventy-two-year-old priest was blessing pictures and medals of the apparition, and urging those of his penitents who felt able to do so to go on pilgrimage to the holy mountain.

Of course the news created an immediate sensation. "What's happened?" everyone wanted to know. "What's made Father Vianney change his mind?"

"There certainly must have been some kind of miracle!"

"That's right. He's never once wanted to talk about La Salette these past eight years."

"And now it's just the opposite!"

"Yes, he doesn't seem to mind talking about it at all."

Gradually the amazing story began to unfold. Recently Father Gerin had paid a visit to Ars and had spoken with Father Vianney about Our Lady's new shrine at La Salette and its importance in the devotional life of the faithful. Seemingly the Holy Spirit had inspired him to use the right words, for immediately upon his return to Grenoble there had been a touching letter from Father Vianney thanking him for his visit.

"What anguish I have been through because of La Salette!" wrote the saintly pastor. "What torments! I was like a man lost in a desert, not knowing which way to turn . . . I begged God to send me some priest from Grenoble who would be able to make my feelings and sufferings his own . . . Now I couldn't have doubts about La Salette if I tried. I asked God for signs that I might believe, and I have obtained them. One may and one ought to believe in La Salette."

Presently there were more details to add to the story. Not only had Father Vianney begged God to send some priest from Grenoble to enlighten him concerning La Salette. Previous to this he had actually forced himself to make an act of faith in the apparition, and had immediately experienced a wonderful peace of mind. Then he had also made a kind of bargain with the Blessed Virgin. If she had really appeared to Melanie and Maximin, if he had really misjudged the lad when he had come to see him eight years ago—well, it was time that everything was set straight. After all, right now his health was very poor and probably he had less than a year to live. How terrible if he went into eternity leaving behind the impression that he had failed to believe in something that was holy, true, beautiful, good!

"Dearest Mother, I need about twelve hundred francs for a certain charity," he prayed. "If you'll let me find the money right away, I'll take that as a sign that you did come to those little ones at La Salette. I'll believe in this with all my heart, and get others to believe, too."

This news created a fresh stir. "Our Lady sent the money?" one person asked another eagerly.

"Of course. No sooner had Father Vianney offered his prayer than he happened to glance toward the mantelpiece. In full sight was almost the entire sum he needed, placed there in his absence by a friend. And the next day another friend made up the balance."

"So that's how Father Vianney came to believe again in La Salette!"

"Yes. Isn't it a wonderful story?"

Everyone agreed. And before the winter storms set in, making travel to the holy mountain both dangerous and impractical, hundreds of former unbelievers had gone there on pilgrimage. Scores of new cures were being reported, too, which caused Bishop Ginoulhiac considerable satisfaction.

"The Devil's done his best to spoil things for us," he reflected, "but without any real success. Maybe now he'll leave us in peace?"

Yet even as the thought crossed his mind, the Bishop smiled ruefully. The Devil and his angels were never idle where a good work was concerned. If they could not permanently thwart Our Lady's cause at La Salette, they could at least continue to hamper it in small but disturbing ways. For instance, there was no doubt that they had succeeded in influencing the minds of those presiding over the lawcourts in Grenoble. In 1854, and again in 1857, Constance Louise Lamerlière had brought suit against the men who had spread the miserable lie that it was she, not Our Lady, who had talked to Melanie and Maximin on September 19, 1846. Hurt and indignant, she had sued her defamers for twenty thousand francs, only to receive an unfavorable verdict in the end and the order to pay the complete costs of both trials.

Then Maximin! What gossip had arisen because it had finally been decided that he had no vocation to the priesthood and ought to withdraw from the Seminary! Now he was working in a Paris hospital, but even there the busy tongues were wagging.

"How could such a stupid young man have been blessed with a heavenly vision?" sneered the enemies of the Church. "Why, he doesn't even know enough to save his wages!"

"That's right. He gives away everything he makes."

"One of these days he'll be nothing but a wretched beggar."

"Wait a minute! Maybe he's not so stupid after all."

"*What?*"

"Maybe he's just pretending to be generous so people will think he's a saint and make a big fuss over him."

"Well, that *is* an idea!"

"And a good one, too. After all, who'd ever let a saint starve? Or be in want of anything?"

"Not the priests or nuns."

"Or any other fool who believes in La Salette."

Such malicious talk naturally irked the Bishop, even though he knew it to be just another trick of the Devil to cast suspicion on Our Lady's apparition to the children.

"At least Melanie doesn't have to suffer from such wicked tongues," he thought gratefully.

Then, in the summer of 1860, came the unexpected blow. After nearly six years in the Carmel at Darlington, for reasons unknown to anyone, twenty-eight-year-old Melanie had asked for a dispensation from her vows! The request had been granted, and at this very moment she was making preparations to return to France.

The Bishop groaned. Melanie had failed a second time as a religious? She was coming back to France as a lay person? How the tongues would wag now!

CHAPTER TWENTY-NINE

THERE WAS a considerable stir when Melanie arrived in France the following month, especially when no details were forthcoming as to why she had left the English Carmelites. And in October, when she went to Marseilles to live with the Sisters of the Compassion (a new community founded by a Jesuit priest named Father Barthes), there was even more excitement.

"Melanie's trying the religious life again!"

"No, she's merely a guest of the Sisters."

"But she's wearing a postulant's black dress and bonnet!"

"Still, she isn't living in the novitiate."

"No, she has her own quarters."

"Maybe she's just going to teach in the Sisters' school."

"Maybe. She always did like that kind of work."

One guess was as good as another, especially in 1861 when Melanie went to Cephalonia, an island off the Greek coast, to help in an orphanage which was under the Sisters' care. Mother Mary of the Presentation, an older member of the community, had been named superior here, and was very pleased with her young helper. But how odd that Melanie should be wearing the same religious habit as her superior! Certainly she had not had time to go through the customary novitiate. Nevertheless, as Sister Zenaïde, she seemed to be an actual member of the community.

Then, to everyone's surprise, Sister Zenaïde returned to Marseilles the following year and entered the Carmelite convent, only to reappear in public ten months later wearing her former semi-religious garb: a plain black dress and bonnet!

"What's going on?" one person asked another curiously. "Why can't Melanie persevere in the religious life? She's thirty-two years old now, and getting to be as unreliable as Maximin."

They could scarcely go further in describing Melanie's unreliability than to compare her with Maximin. After just a short stay in the Paris hospital, he had told certain friends he would like to have more education. Through their kindness, he had been able to spend three terms in a local college. Then presently he had decided to be a doctor, and had put in two long and difficult years in medical school. Now in 1864, convinced that he would never be able

MELANIE WAS BACK IN FRANCE!

to pass the required examinations for his degree, he was considering a totally different career. He would join the Papal Zouaves, a group of French military men who had pledged themselves to defend the Holy Father in time of danger.

Bishop Ginoulhiac was at a loss to explain the eccentric behavior of his young charges. Of course neither Melanie nor Maximin had ever given any real cause for scandal. They were far more prayerful and devout than appeared on the surface. But in 1867, after Melanie had joined the Sisters of the Compassion in Marseilles for still another time, then left the community to travel in Italy, he was genuinely disturbed. The cause of Our Lady of La Salette was prospering, with thousands of pilgrims coming every year to pray at her new shrine. But the gossip about Melanie and Maximin nevertheless had its effect. Without doubt there would be many more to believe in Our Lady's apparition if only these two would lead more regular lives.

"Never mind, Your Lordship," said the Bishop's advisers. "Even if the worst happened, and Melanie and Maximin should turn out to be great sinners, it wouldn't alter the fact that Our Lady did give the world an important message through them. But we also have to remember that their part in things is long since finished. They said as much themselves sixteen years ago."

"Sixteen years ago?"

"Yes, in 1851, after they had written their secrets for Pope Pius the Ninth. They both declared then that their work was done. They seemed very happy and relieved about it, too, as though from now on their lives would be their own."

The Bishop was thoughtful. If only he could talk to Bishop de Bruillard about all this! But he had died seven years ago, shortly after Melanie's return from England. Even now his tomb in the Cathedral of Grenoble was a place of pilgrimage, while his heart, taken to the holy mountain at his own request, was one of the most cherished possessions of the Missionaries of La Salette. As for Fathers Rousselot and Gerin, who had presented the children's secrets to Pope Pius on July 18, 1851? They also had passed away. Actually there were not too many people living now, of those who had been originally concerned with a study of the apparition, to offer advice and encouragement.

However, the Bishop tried not to be unduly disturbed about present difficulties. After all, the building of Our Lady's shrine at La Salette was an enormous undertaking, and finances a continual problem. Then recently another project had been occupying his mind: the founding of a new religious community to care for women pilgrims who came to the holy mountain. Since 1855 the Sisters of Providence had been in charge of this work, but they were primarily a teaching community and badly needed in their own schools and orphanages.

"The Missionaries of La Salette, priests and Brothers alike, have done wonderful things for Our Lady's cause since 1852," reflected the Bishop. "But we do need some Sisters of La Salette as well. Now, who's to start such a group? And when?"

For a while it seemed that these questions must go unanswered. Then presently Mademoiselle Deluy-Fabry, a pious woman from Marseilles, came forward with an idea. She and a few friends had long thought of consecrating themselves to God's service in a community especially dedicated to the Blessed Virgin. Perhaps, if the Bishop were willing, they could be the first Sisters of Our Lady of La Salette?

Bishop Ginoulhiac was delighted at such a suggestion. And in 1869, when the would-be foundress returned from Rome with the blessing of Pope Pius the Ninth on the proposed venture, he assigned the Vicar General of the diocese to draw up a rule for the new community. He himself would try to find further candidates.

However, in 1870 there was a change in plans. Bishop Ginoulhiac found himself unexpectedly elevated to the important post of Archbishop of Lyons. It was not to be his privilege after all but that of Monsignor Paulinier, his successor, to guide the fortunes of the new community.

CHAPTER THIRTY

ALTHOUGH HE realized it was a great honor to be appointed to the See of Grenoble, Bishop Paulinier assumed his new duties with considerable reluctance. What a responsibility to be placed in charge of one of the most famous shrines in Europe! Of course much progress had been made in the building of Our Lady's new church since the first stone had been laid eighteen years ago, but there was still an enormous amount of work to be done. The isolated location of La Salette made the task even more difficult, plus the fact that supplies could be brought up the mountainside during five months of the year only, when the winter snows had melted and all danger from avalanches had passed. Then, too, over what rugged trails the workmen had to haul the great blocks of marble and granite, the timber, sand, steel and other materials! It was a terribly slow and costly process, even in the best of weather.

Also, Melanie and Maximin were still a problem. Maximin, now thirty-five years old, had recently joined the regular French army, and now was stationed at a barracks near Grenoble. Thirty-nine-year-old Melanie was still in Italy, with Mother Mary of the Presentation her constant companion. Bishop Xavier Petagna of Castellamare was doing what he could for the two women, but he was a poor man, and frequently they were forced to travel about and look for other benefactors. Realizing this, Father Giraud, the superior of the Missionaries of La Salette, often sent Melanie generous sums of money. And from time to time he helped other members of her family, too.

Bishop Paulinier was baffled. Why had Melanie gone to Italy in the first place? Who was Bishop Petagna? As for Mother Mary of the Presentation, why wasn't she at home in her convent in Marseilles with the rest of her community? Why had she taken upon herself such a singular life of insecurity and hardship?

Investigation revealed that in 1867, after she had spent three years with them as Sister Mary Victor, the Sisters of the Compassion had decided that Melanie did not have a vocation to their way of life. Distraught, the young woman had appealed for help to Bishop Petagna, a visitor at the Motherhouse in Marseilles. The Bishop, who had known her for some time, took an immediate interest in Melanie and her plight, and suggested that she come to Italy where she might be able to help him establish a new teaching community.

However, Mother Mary of the Presentation was rather doubtful about such a venture. She had been Melanie's loyal friend for seven years, ever since the time when the young woman had sought refuge with the community upon her return from England. In fact, Father Barthes himself had asked her to take a personal interest in Melanie—to be a mother to her, so to speak. She had followed these orders, and very soon had become deeply attached to her young charge. Repeatedly she had defended her when other members of the community complained about her odd ways, her lack of cooperation, her strange spells of moodiness. Even more. She had refused to admit that Melanie did not have a vocation to the Sisters of the Compassion. The poor child was always being misunderstood by those who ought to know better, she insisted. It was a cruel and heartless thing to send her out alone into the world. After all, hadn't Melanie seen and talked to the Blessed Virgin? How imprudent to pass judgment on such a privileged soul! And what a pity that Father Barthes was not still alive! He would never have permitted her to be treated so unfairly.

"To make a long story short, Your Lordship, Mother Mary felt it was her duty to continue looking after Melanie," explained the Bishop's advisers. "The authorities in Marseilles finally gave permission for her to take the girl to Italy, while still retaining membership in her own community. Presumably she'll be there until Bishop Petagna has established his new teaching group."

Bishop Paulinier looked a little puzzled. "But when's that going to be?" he demanded. "After all, it's three years since Melanie left France. Hasn't anything definite been done in all this time?"

The advisers shook their heads. "No, Your Lordship. Seemingly there's been one difficulty after another in starting the proposed community."

For a moment Bishop Paulinier was silent. It was true that not so long ago, owing to political troubles in their homeland, many of the Italian clergy had sought refuge in France. Apparently the generous founder of the Sisters of the Compassion had given the first of these unfortunates a haven at the Motherhouse in Marseilles. Then, when Bishop Petagna had come along, he had helped him, too. And also Melanie. But now that the good-hearted priest was dead, and times in Italy somewhat improved—

"This whole affair is certainly most involved," he declared finally. "I guess all we can do is to pray that things work out in the end."

By 1871, however, there were other matters to claim the Bishop's prayerful attention. Mademoiselle Deluy-Fabry had now secured five members for the proposed community of the Sisters of Our Lady of La Salette, as well as a temporary headquarters in Grenoble. Since the Vicar General had completed the rule, and since everyone was anxious to enter upon their new way of life, perhaps Bishop Paulinier would set a date for the reception of the habit?

The Bishop did not have to reflect long in order to make a choice. "The Feast of the Seven Sorrows of Our Lady would be the most appropriate day," he decided.

So on September 17, 1871, in the Sisters' temporary convent in Grenoble, Mademoiselle Deluy-Fabry and her five companions received their new religious dress. Then on August 16, 1872, at an imposing Motherhouse which had just been acquired outside the city, five more young women were received into the community.

"Eleven Sisters of La Salette!" exclaimed the Bishop, delighted beyond words that so much had been accomplished in the two short years he had spent in Grenoble. "What a splendid beginning!"

However, on December 14 there was even more rejoicing when the six original members made their first vows and left soon after for their new quarters on the holy mountain. At last the busy Missionaries of La Salette had their longed-for helpers! And the Sisters of Providence could also rejoice. For after having faithfully cared for the needs of women pilgrims during the past seventeen years, they were now free to return to their own important work in the schools and orphanages of the diocese.

CHAPTER THIRTY-ONE

B Y THE spring of 1873, the Sisters of La Salette were endearing themselves to all who visited the holy mountain. How devoted they were to the pilgrims, especially to the sick! How eager to be of use!

"It's just as though the Blessed Virgin herself were caring for us," one person told another.

Father Giraud, the superior of the Missionary Fathers, was deeply grateful for this latest blessing. Now that the Sisters had come, there were even more zealous helpers to promote Our Lady's cause. And since 1858, when he had first joined the Missionary Fathers, this had always been the work closest to his heart. Never had he spared any effort to explain to people that Our Lady is the Reconciler as well as the Refuge of Sinners—the beautiful and all-powerful

Mother who constantly pleads with her Son to have mercy on a sinful world.

"She really meant what she told the children," he often reflected. "People *must* turn away from sin and mend their lives, otherwise terrible things are going to happen."

However, even as he urged the pilgrims to heed Our Lady's message—particularly to keep Sundays holy and to refrain from bad language—he experienced a certain uneasiness. Surely it would be far less difficult to convince the world of the importance of Our Lady's words if the secrets of Melanie and Maximin could be made known? More than twenty years had passed since they had been confided to Pope Pius the Ninth, and in all that time His Holiness had never seen fit to publish them. Now that he was in his eighties, and his health none too good. . . .

"Perhaps someone ought to ask him about the secrets," Father Giraud decided one day. "If we wait much longer, it may be too late."

But who was to undertake such a delicate task? In the end, on the occasion of a trip to Rome, Father Giraud found himself at the Vatican on this very mission. But when he had respectfully made known his request to Pope Pius, the aged pontiff merely smiled.

"You want to know the secrets of La Salette?" he asked kindly. "Well, here they are, my son: 'Unless you do penance, you shall all perish.'"

Father Giraud was keenly disappointed at this vague reply, but he did not press for further details.

After all, it was only too evident that the Holy Father did not think it wise to share the secrets with anyone. Unless something unforeseen happened, he would carry them with him to the grave.

"Well, there's no use in worrying," he decided. "His Holiness certainly knows what's best for all of us."

However, there were many people who could not so readily set their curiosity aside. And in the fall of 1874, when it became known that Maximin was not in the best of health, considerable gossip arose concerning him.

"Maximin's got only a year to live!" one person told another excitedly. "Maybe less than that!"

"That's right. And they do say he's going to tell his secret before he dies!"

"Did you hear he's also writing a book about La Salette and keeping nothing back?"

"No! Surely Maximin hasn't the patience to write a book!"

"Of course not. And how foolish to say he's going to die when he's only thirty-nine!"

"But he *is* sick . . . from tuberculosis or heart trouble or something."

"Then why doesn't he ask Our Lady to cure him?"

"Well. . . ."

"Maybe he's just pretending to be sick so he won't have to work."

"But he doesn't have to work! The Jourdain family in Corps have been supporting him for years."

"No, the Jourdains lost all their money long ago."

"That's right. Maximin's been supporting them."

"But how could he, when he's never stayed long enough in one place to save anything?"

"You forget that he's built up quite a business in religious goods at Corps—medals and pictures of the apparition and so forth. All the pilgrims like to buy from him."

"Maybe so. But he still can't make very much from that kind of work."

"No. He'd do far better with a book about La Salette."

"Especially if he decided to write about his secret."

For several weeks these and other confusing rumors persisted. Then early in November a new story began to make the rounds. Maximin was coming from Corps to spend a few days at Our Lady's shrine, hoping to be cured of his various ailments.

The Sisters of La Salette were as excited as anyone else at the news. Being comparative newcomers to the holy mountain, they had never seen Maximin. And now, most unexpectedly—

"We must try to learn all we can from him about Our Lady's visit," they told one another eagerly.

Thus on November 4, when Maximin arrived on the holy mountain, he was immediately surrounded by an earnest little group who could not do enough to make him welcome. The pilgrims who happened to be present were also beside themselves with eagerness. And with relief, too, for Maximin was in much better health than they had expected. True, he was

"SHE WAS BRIGHTER THAN THE SUN. . . ."

thin and a bit pale. But he was able to walk about. And he seemed to be in excellent spirits. God willing, he would tell them, as well as the Sisters, all about Our Lady's apparition. And about the book he was writing, too.

Even though he was now thirty-nine years old, Maximin still retained many of the impetuous ways of his childhood. Thus, no sooner did he learn how anxious the Sisters were to hear about the apparition than he set about satisfying their desires. Then, at the pilgrims' request, he led a large group to all the places of interest on the holy mountain, explaining and describing everything that had happened there twenty-eight years before.

For instance, here was the exact spot where two little shepherds had first seen Our Lady seated, weeping bitterly, surrounded by a dazzling light. When they had approached, she had risen to her feet and told them not to be afraid.

"She was very tall, sir?" ventured one of the pilgrims.

"Oh, yes. Tall and majestic like a queen. And so very beautiful!"

"It's true that she didn't cast any shadow, even though the sun was shining?"

"That's right. She was brighter than the sun. And though she had the form of a beautiful lady, somehow she was like crystal. We could see right through her."

This detail amazed a number of those present who had never heard it before. "Weren't you and Melanie frightened at that, sir? After all, to be able to look right through a person. . . ."

Maximin smiled and shook his head. "No, we were never afraid after Our Lady spoke to us. You see, she was so kind and motherly. Then, too, we were worried about why she was so sad."

"She stayed with you half an hour?"

"About that time."

"Then she began to disappear?"

"Yes. Over there, a few yards to the right."

Everyone looked to where Maximin pointed, noting at the same time how his voice had suddenly taken on a note of sadness.

"You . . . you felt bad when Our Lady left, sir? You tried to keep her from going?"

"Oh, yes! Of course at first we didn't realize that she actually was going. But when she had risen about a yard into the air and her head had vanished from sight, then her arms. . . ."

"Yes, yes, sir! What did you do?"

Maximin smiled thoughtfully. "Why, I remember jumping as high as I could to try to catch some of the flowers on her shoes. But I grabbed at nothing. Our Lady had gone, leaving only a wonderful brightness in the air. A moment later, that also had disappeared."

"They say your dog was with you at the time, sir. Is that true?"

"Yes. Loulou was along."

"And what did she do during the time of the apparition?"

Maximin shrugged. "Nothing. She never once barked at Our Lady, or made any kind of fuss, although she was a restless little creature who didn't care for strangers."

Needless to say, for the rest of the day no one could talk about anything but Maximin's disclosures. What a privilege to have heard the amazing story from his very lips! To have been able to go with him about the holy mountain! Of course it was disappointing to discover that he was not writing a book about La Salette after all; that he possessed only a few pages of random notes about his childhood and its great experience, and that he had absolutely no intention of telling his secret to anyone.

"Still, we did learn a great deal about Our Lady's visit," one pilgrim told another.

"Yes. And now we really ought to try to repay Maximin for his kindness."

"But how? By money?"

"Oh, no! Prayer would be the best way. After all, hasn't he come here to ask Our Lady for good health? Maybe if we join our prayers to his, she'll grant that request."

CHAPTER THIRTY-TWO

E VERYONE DID pray hard for Maximin's cure. And presently, when he left the holy mountain to return to his home in Corps, it seemed that he was considerably better. But four months later, on March 1, 1875, there was distressing news. Maximin's strange and troubled career was over. The best of medical care had been of no avail.

Madame Jourdain and her husband (who had been Maximin's benefactors for many years), were beside themselves with grief. Maximin had had a beautiful and edifying death, but this did not alter the fact that they had lost one who was like a son to them. To make matters worse, they were both old and tired, and business reverses had long since robbed them of their savings. Now that Maximin was gone, their only means of support had also disappeared, for very few pilgrims seemed interested in purchasing religious articles at their little shop.

"We have nothing now," they mourned. "Absolutely nothing. . . ."

The Missionaries of La Salette were deeply touched at the Jourdains' plight, particularly when they learned that the aged couple spent much of their time in the cemetery of Corps where Maximin was buried. Accordingly, they sent gifts of food and money as often as they could. And whenever the two managed to make a pilgrimage to Our Lady's shrine (where Maximin had asked that his heart be buried), they did everything to comfort and console them.

However, the Missionaries were not a little disturbed when Madame Jourdain presently announced that she and her husband had found a way out of their financial difficulties. Maximin had left them the various notes he had made about his early life. With some editing, these could be turned into a really worthwhile book.

"Fathers, everybody would like to read such a story," declared Madame Jourdain excitedly. "And if I add a part about Maximin's life with us, that'll make it even more interesting. Why, we can probably sell thousands of copies without the least bit of trouble!"

Father Giraud was not so sure. "Perhaps," he said cautiously. "But of course nothing should appear in print without Bishop Paulinier's permission."

"Oh, no, Father," agreed Madame Jourdain enthusiastically. "That's understood."

However, by the time the new book was finished, Bishop Paulinier had been transferred to Besançon and Bishop Fava, from the island of Martinique in the French West Indies, had taken his place. And from the first he was extremely doubtful as to the worth of Madame Jourdain's manuscript. Of course the old lady had done her best to write an interesting story, but it was only too evident that she had neither the skill nor the experience necessary for such a work. In fact, her description of Maximin's later life left much to be desired. Not only had she seen fit to pass over his many faults and present him as a saint and a hero. Because of a failing memory, she had also made several errors as to time and place.

"It really wouldn't be wise to have such a book published, Your Lordship," was the decision of the Bishop's advisers, as well as of the Missionaries of La Salette. "It isn't based on truth. And it has no literary value at all."

Bishop Fava hesitated. "You mean the part Madame Jourdain wrote?"

"Yes, and even the part Maximin wrote."

"But surely the good man described his own life accurately!"

"Frankly, no, Your Lordship. The notes he left with the Jourdains were only careless jottings. They certainly don't agree with the statements he made when he was young."

After some deliberation, Bishop Fava and the Missionaries of La Salette decided to have nothing to do with Madame Jourdain's manuscript. Naturally the old lady was disappointed, for she had spent more than two years working on her story, and the money from its sale would have meant so much.

"This new Bishop from the French West Indies just doesn't understand!" she sobbed when the rejected manuscript reached her. "Why, he never even knew Maximin! And now he thinks he can tell me what happened and didn't happen when the poor boy lived with us!"

A number of friends agreed that the Bishop was ill-informed. And prejudiced, too. The new book was very interesting and ought to be published. After all, hadn't Maximin suffered for years from cruel and malicious tongues? It was high time that someone took his part and told the truth about him—how generous he had been to the poor, how devoted to Our Lady, how eager to be a missionary priest. . . .

"No one knew Maximin quite like you did," they told Madame Jourdain sympathetically. "Why don't you have the book published in spite of Bishop Fava and the Missionary Fathers? It would certainly do a lot of good."

The old lady hesitated. "Oh, but that wouldn't be right!"

"Of course it'd be right. And think of all the money you'd make, Madame! Why, in just a little while you'd be able to pay off all your debts and never again be a burden to anyone. Wouldn't that be fine?"

"B-but—"

"There, there, don't worry. You've written a wonderful story. We'll help you get it into print."

Of course Bishop Fava was worried when he learned that Madame Jourdain was letting herself be persuaded into submitting her work to a publisher. Then presently there was even greater cause for anxiety. In November, 1879, word arrived from Italy that forty-eight-year-old Melanie had also written a story about herself. It had just been published and bore an *Imprimatur* from Bishop Zola of Leece. But it was not merely an account of her life. Incorporated in the text was what she claimed to be her famous secret, which, she insisted, Our Lady had long ago given her permission to tell!

The news created an immediate sensation throughout all Europe, and there was a mad scramble to procure copies. As a result, in a matter of weeks several conflicting tales were making the rounds.

"Melanie says Antichrist is here!"

"No, no, he's not coming for another hundred years!"

"Priests and nuns aren't living as they should!"

"That's right. They're too interested in making money!"

"No, it's the Bishops and Cardinals who are at fault. They don't have any real interest in becoming saints."

"If they'd only practice the True Devotion to the Blessed Virgin Mary of Father Louis Grignion De Montfort, things would be different."

"Because they won't, terrible trials are in store for the Church."

"Yes, there's going to be another war!"

"And famine!"

"And pestilence!"

"Oh, but that's not what I heard!"

"No, indeed. Melanie says we're going to have peace."

"Yes. Our Lady's well pleased with all of us."

Bishop Fava was beside himself over such disturbing gossip, particularly when he discovered there were good grounds for believing that Melanie was not herself mentally. What she had written *might* be the secret, but then again it might be only the product of an overwrought imagination. More than twenty-seven years ago, when she had been living with the Sisters of Providence in Corenc, she had written a short life of herself which had contained all manner of surprising statements. For instance, that the apparition of Our Lady on September 19, 1846, was only one of many similar heavenly favors which she had enjoyed; that she had often been granted glimpses of Paradise; that in her own childhood the Child Jesus had been her almost constant companion; that she had even received the stigmata at the age of three!

At first the little autobiography had aroused considerable interest among the superiors. Later, when Melanie began to suffer from her strange spells of moodiness, then left the community in 1854, the story was set aside as worthless, and all but forgotten. Now, however, in 1879, when she was living in the world and everyone was aware that her newly published work bore an *Imprimatur* from Bishop Zola, a generous benefactor since the death of Bishop Petagna—

"It's all most confusing," declared Bishop Fava's advisers. "And it's certainly not going to help Our Lady's cause at La Salette."

The Bishop was forced to agree. The enemies of the Church had long since profited from the eccentric behavior of Melanie and Maximin to cast suspicion on everything connected with the apparition. Now that the so-called secret was being accepted by some and rejected by others, with much bitterness and misunderstanding as the result. . . .

"We'll just have to wait until we hear from Rome about the whole affair," he decided. "God willing, someone in authority there will make a statement soon."

CHAPTER THIRTY-THREE

IN DUE course word did come from Cardinal Caterini, in the name of the Sacred Congregation of the Holy Office, that Melanie's work was not looked upon favorably at Rome and that all existing copies should be withdrawn from circulation. However, in many quarters this only served to stimulate an unhealthy curiosity, and soon new copies began to appear in both France and Italy. Well-meaning people, including numerous priests, were divided in opinion concerning the whole affair, so that once again La Salette became a stormy issue. Then in 1881, when Madame Jourdain's work, *Maximin, as Described by Himself,* was published, there was even more confusion.

"What a pity that Pope Pius the Ninth is dead!" one person told another. "He'd surely be able to do something about all this because he knew both the secrets."

"Well, maybe Pope Leo the Thirteenth knows them, too, and will make some statement soon," was the hopeful suggestion.

But Pope Leo (who had taken office in 1878, one year before the publication of the so-called secret), did not see fit to commit himself, and little by little excitement about the whole affair began to die down. However, the enemies of the Church continued their slanderous attacks upon Melanie. She was a mad woman, they said, who had never seen the Blessed Virgin, much less heard her speak or been given a message by her. As a result, the pilgrimages to La Salette were pointless and uncalled-for. Indeed, the shrine was only a money-making venture on the part of the Bishops of Grenoble, the Missionary Fathers and the Sisters.

As the years passed, there were more and more efforts to discredit La Salette. The fact that Melanie never seemed to live long in one place, passing back and forth from Italy to France, was a point of constant criticism. If she was really a holy person, people said, why didn't she settle down in a convent, or at least devote herself to some charitable work? Why was she always on the move? And why did she cause so much unrest by repeated references to certain terrifying statements in her so-called secret?

Bishop Fava was distressed by all the unfortunate gossip, likewise Bishop Henry who succeeded him in 1899. Then presently things were even more confused when sixty-nine-year-old Melanie wrote another account of her life. This story recorded the same kind of extraordinary events as the one she had written while living with the Sisters of Providence in Corenc. Once again there were references to a childhood filled with all kinds of heavenly favors, which left the impression that the author was one of the most spiritually blessed of living creatures.

What to do? Bishop Henry finally decided to ignore the new book entirely. Melanie was a good and pious woman, and there was no doubt that she had suffered a great deal from injustice and persecution. But she was also emotionally unstable, and there was no use in taking her various writings too seriously. After all, her official connection with La Salette had ended in July, 1851, when she had written her secret for Pope Pius the Ninth. She had said as much herself at the time. What a pity that since then she had frequently been influenced to the contrary! More than once this had caused a widespread doubt concerning Our Lady's apparition at La Salette, especially in foreign countries where explanatory details were lacking.

"And that's just what the Devil wants," reflected Bishop Henry sadly. "He'll do everything he can to keep people from loving Our Lady and praying to her."

Upon the death of Pope Leo the Thirteenth in 1903, there was renewed speculation as to whether his successor, Pope Pius the Tenth, would make some public statement regarding the so-called secret which Melanie had published in 1879. Was it authentic or not? After all, what a vast amount of trouble the world had known since 1846! Couldn't it be that these catastrophes—famine, flood, pestilence—were connected in some way with a failure to heed Our Lady's warning at La Salette? Then, too, how many wars there had been! In Mexico, the Crimea, India, Italy, America, Denmark, Austria, France, Prussia; between Russia and Turkey, China and Japan, Spain and America, the South Africans and the British. . . .

However, as his predecessors had done, Pope Pius the Tenth refrained from all public comment, and once again the storm over La Salette began to subside. By 1904 comparatively few people even knew what had become of Melanie. Presumably she was still traveling about somewhere, either in Italy or in France, living on alms and doing what she could to publicize her so-called secret, To some extent this was true, but in the summer of 1904 there was considerable gossip among the residents of Altamura, a town near Bari, in southeastern Italy. A quiet, elderly woman, wearing shabby black clothes, had just arrived to make her home with the wealthy Gianuzzi family at the invitation of Bishop Cecchini.

"It's Melanie!" one person told another excitedly. "There's no doubt about that!"

In vain the Bishop tried to conceal the identity of the guest, so that she would be spared publicity. Despite his best efforts, however, it was soon common knowledge that the silent, black-clad stranger who assisted so devoutly at Mass each morning in the Cathedral was Melanie Mathieu of La Salette. But how worn she looked' How tired' Far older than her seventy-three years. . . .

"Poor thing, she doesn't seem a bit well," was the general opinion. "All this traveling about has been too much for her."

As the weeks passed, the people of Altamura were much impressed by Melanie's prayerful life. Soon many were wondering if she wasn't a saint. And in September, when she left the Gianuzzis and retired to a small room in a poor part of town, a number were convinced of it. Although she rarely spoke to anyone, and was to be seen only in the early morning on her way to and from Mass at the Cathedral, what a beautiful smile she had for all who greeted her' Somehow there was something heavenly about it, as though she were still seeing the Blessed Mother. Then, too, there was the report of the landlady that Melanie's entire day was spent in prayer and pious reading, that she slept upon the bare floor, and that her only nourishment was the light breakfast she took at the Bishop's house each morning after Mass.

Gradually many began frequenting the Cathedral just to profit from the sight of Melanie's great devotion. But on the morning of December 15, the octave day of the Feast of the Immaculate Conception, these worshipers looked at one another in dismay. Melanie's place was empty!

"She's gone away somewhere like she always does," they thought. "We'll never see her again."

However, when word was brought to Bishop Cecchini that Melanie had not assisted at Mass as usual, an expression of concern crossed his face. At once a servant was sent to see what was the trouble. But in just a little while the man was back with the news that Melanie's shutters were drawn, the door locked, and that there had been no response to his vigorous knocking.

"Something's wrong," declared the Bishop, now more worried than ever. "Melanie would never miss hearing Mass without a good cause. We'd better call the police."

Soon an anxious little group had gathered in the hallway outside Melanie's humble quarters. Repeated shouts and knocking having had no effect, the door was forced and an entry made. Whereupon there was a gasp of dismay. Seventy-three-year-old Melanie, neatly dressed, her arms folded across her breast, her eyes closed, an especially happy smile upon her lips, was lying dead upon the floor!

"I . . . I knew it!" burst out Pascal Massari, one of the bystanders. "She died last night, after the angels sang and brought her Holy Communion!"

Everyone looked up in amazement. *"What?"*

"Yes, it's true," put in an awestruck woman neighbor. "I heard that beautiful singing. And the tinkling of the little bell, too. But I never thought . . . oh, Mother of God! This *is* a miracle!"

CHAPTER THIRTY-FOUR

SOON THE whole town of Altamura was buzzing with excitement. Two of Melanie's neighbors were ready to swear that they had heard
angelic voices singing the *Pange Lingua* the night
before her death! The sound had been incredibly soft
and sweet, as though coming from a great distance,
and had been heard right after the evening Angelus.
It had continued for several minutes, to be followed
by a moment's silence. Then had come the tinkling of
a small bell, as though a priest were bringing Holy
Communion to a dying person. But no priest had been
abroad in the streets at such an hour. As for any local
singers rendering the beautiful Eucharistic hymn of
Holy Thursday. . . .

"That's impossible," was the general opinion.
"Those were no earthly voices that sang the *Pange*

Lingua. They came from heaven itself to welcome Melanie home."

In Grenoble, Bishop Henry heard about all this with mixed feelings. Of course it was not impossible that Melanie's last moments had been miraculously blessed. On the other hand, it would never do to say so officially. Always the Church moved very cautiously in such affairs. Indeed, whole centuries frequently elapsed before she formally passed upon the sanctity of her children. Right now the main thing for everyone to remember, and for which to be grateful, was that Melanie had always lived a good life, and Maximin, too. Both could well serve as models for several of their critics. After all, what sufferings they had endured from cruel and malicious tongues! And from poverty and ill health as well. Certainly December 15, 1904, and March 1, 1875, the dates of their respective deaths, would always be remembered by anyone who had a real interest in La Salette.

"May Melanie and Maximin both rest in peace!" was the Bishop's frequent and heartfelt prayer.

But even as he remembered the souls of those who had been so intimately connected with Our Lady's apparition, the names of other faithful workers came to mind, too. Bishop de Bruillard, Father Gerin, Father Rousselot, Bishop Ginoulhiac, Father Mélin, Bishop Paulinier, Father Louis Joseph Perrin, Bishop Fava ... ah, how many there had been to promote the cause of Our Lady of La Salette! God willing, these dear departed ones would be replaced by equally

"OUR LADY'S MESSAGE WILL NEVER GROW OLD. . . ."

zealous lovers of Mary. For though it had been fifty-eight years since Our Lady had appeared on the holy mountain, her message was still as vital as ever. People must turn away from sin and do penance, otherwise dreadful trials would come upon the world.

"That message will never grow old," thought the Bishop. "Even if Our Lady should come to earth again, it will surely be to tell us much the same thing." And as he reflected upon all this, familiar words began to echo in the Bishop's mind; encouraging words, words spoken by the kindest and best of Mothers:

"Come near, my children. And don't be afraid. I am here to tell you great news. . . ."

St. Meinrad, Indiana
Feast of Our Lady of Mount Carmel
July 16, 1951

Our Lady of La Salette,

reconciler of sinners,

pray without ceasing for us

who have recourse to thee.

An indulgence of 300 days
(S.P. Ap., November 7, 1927, and December 12, 1933).

 TAN·BOOKS

TAN Books is the Publisher You Can Trust With Your Faith.

TAN Books was founded in 1967 to preserve the spiritual, intellectual, and liturgical traditions of the Catholic Church. At a critical moment in history TAN kept alive the great classics of the Faith and drew many to the Church. In 2008 TAN was acquired by Saint Benedict Press. Today TAN continues to teach and defend the Faith to a new generation of readers.

TAN publishes more than 600 booklets, Bibles, and books. Popular subject areas include theology and doctrine, prayer and the supernatural, history, biography, and the lives of the saints. TAN's line of educational and homeschooling resources is featured at TANHomeschool.com.

TAN publishes under several imprints, including TAN, Neumann Press, ACS Books, and the Confraternity of the Precious Blood. Sister imprints include Saint Benedict Press, Catholic Courses, and Catholic Scripture Study.

**For more information about TAN,
or to request a free catalog, visit
TANBooks.com**

**Or call us toll-free at
(800) 437-5876**